CAMBRIDGE LIBRARY COLLECTION

Books of enduring scholarly value

History

The books reissued in this series include accounts of historical events and movements by eye-witnesses and contemporaries, as well as landmark studies that assembled significant source materials or developed new historiographical methods. The series includes work in social, political and military history on a wide range of periods and regions, giving modern scholars ready access to influential publications of the past.

The African Slave Trade

Sir Thomas Fowell Buxton (1786–1845) was a committed social reformer throughout his life and became involved with the abolition of slavery during his time as an M.P., taking over the leadership of the abolition movement in the British House of Commons after William Wilberforce retired in 1825. Following the abolition of slavery in Britain and its colonies in 1833, and his loss of his Parliamentary seat in 1837, Buxton concerned himself with the slave trade along the African coast still perpetrated by Africans, Arabs and the Portuguese. The results of his research and conclusions were originally published in 1839, and demonstrate the extent to which slave trading still existed, and its human cost in mortality and misery, despite attempts at policing by the British navy. Buxton explores the theory that the key to complete abolition is a change in market economics to eliminate the need for African slave labour.

T0381743

Cambridge University Press has long been a pioneer in the reissuing of out-of-print titles from its own backlist, producing digital reprints of books that are still sought after by scholars and students but could not be reprinted economically using traditional technology. The Cambridge Library Collection extends this activity to a wider range of books which are still of importance to researchers and professionals, either for the source material they contain, or as landmarks in the history of their academic discipline.

Drawing from the world-renowned collections in the Cambridge University Library, and guided by the advice of experts in each subject area, Cambridge University Press is using state-of-the-art scanning machines in its own Printing House to capture the content of each book selected for inclusion. The files are processed to give a consistently clear, crisp image, and the books finished to the high quality standard for which the Press is recognised around the world. The latest print-on-demand technology ensures that the books will remain available indefinitely, and that orders for single or multiple copies can quickly be supplied.

The Cambridge Library Collection will bring back to life books of enduring scholarly value (including out-of-copyright works originally issued by other publishers) across a wide range of disciplines in the humanities and social sciences and in science and technology.

The African Slave Trade

Thomas Fowell Buxton

CAMBRIDGE UNIVERSITY PRESS

Cambridge, New York, Melbourne, Madrid, Cape Town, Singapore,
São Paolo, Delhi, Dubai, Tokyo, Mexico City

Published in the United States of America by Cambridge University Press, New York

www.cambridge.org
Information on this title: www.cambridge.org/9781108027687

© in this compilation Cambridge University Press 2010

This edition first published 1839
This digitally printed version 2010

ISBN 978-1-108-02768-7 Paperback

THE

AFRICAN SLAVE TRADE.

BY

THOMAS FOWELL BUXTON, Esq.

" This is a people robbed and spoiled; they are all of them snared in holes, and they are hid in prison houses: they are for a prey, and none delivereth; for a spoil, and none saith, Restore."— *Isaiah*, xlii. 22.

SECOND EDITION.

LONDON:
JOHN MURRAY, ALBEMARLE-STREET.

MDCCCXXXIX.

London:
Printed by WILLIAM CLOWES and SONS,
Stamford-street.

CONTENTS.

b 2

INTRODUCTION.

No one possessing any knowledge of, or anxiety on the subject of the Negro race can fail to deplore the present state of Africa.

Desirous to ascertain why it is, that all our gigantic efforts and costly sacrifices for the suppression of the Slave Trade have proved unavailing, I have employed some leisure time in surveying this whole subject, and in tracing out, as far as I have been able, the true cause of our failure. My original impression was, that, in increased efforts at sea, and in reducing Portugal to the necessity of executing her engagements with us, the effective remedy was to be found, and that little more than these would be required for the gratification of the ardent desire felt by the British nation for the abolition of the Slave Trade. But a closer scrutiny into the facts of the case has conducted me to a different conclusion. There are, I now think, reasonable grounds for believing, that we should still be disappointed, although we were to double our naval force engaged in that ranch of service, and although it were resolved to take the most peremptory measures with Portugal.

I do not underrate the value of our maritime exertions. I think it may be good policy, and, in the long run, true economy, to multiply the number of our vessels, to do at once and by a blow all that can be done in this way ; to increase our expenses for a few years, in order to escape the necessity of incurring cost, not materially less, for an indefinite period. Neither do I wish that our government should address Portugal in any terms short of a declaration, that our cruisers will have orders to seize, after a fixed and an early day, every vessel under Portuguese colours engaged in the slave-traffic, to bring the crew to trial as pirates, and inflict upon them the severest secondary punishment which our law allows. Decisive measures of this kind would, there is no doubt, facilitate our success, by removing some of the great impediments which stand in the way of other remedial measures ; nevertheless, I am compelled, by the various evidence which it has been my province to examine, to place my main reliance, not on the employment of force, but on the encouragement which we may be able to give to the legitimate commerce and the agricultural cultivation of Africa.

We attempt to put down the Slave Trade " by the strong hand" alone ; and this is, I apprehend, the cause of our failure. Our system, in many respects too feeble, is in one sense too bold. The African has acquired a taste for the productions of the civilised world. They have become essential to him. The parent,—debased and brutalised as he is,—barters his child; the chief his subject; each individual looks with an evil eye on his neighbour, and lays snares to catch him,—because the sale of children, subjects, and neighbours, is the only means as yet afforded, by European commerce, for the supply of those wants which that commerce has created. To say that the African, under present circumstances, shall not deal in man, is to say that he shall long in vain for his accustomed gratifications. The tide, thus pent up, will break its way over every barrier. In order effectually to divert the stream from the direction which it has hitherto taken, we must open another, a safer, and a more convenient channel. When we shall have experimentally convinced the African that it is in his power to obtain his supplies in more than their usual abundance, by honest means, then, and not till then, we may expect that he will be reconciled to the abolition of the Slave Trade.

This work does not fully carry into effect the design with which it was commenced. To a description of the extent and horrors of the Slave Trade, the failure of our efforts for its suppression, and the capabilities of Africa for legitimate commerce, I had intended to add some practical suggestions for calling forth the latent energies of that quarter of the globe, and for exhibiting to its inhabitants where their true interest lies.

Upon consideration it appeared that a premature disclosure of these suggestions might be inconvenient; I therefore withhold that part of my subject for the present, with the intention of resuming it hereafter; but, although I am disabled from entering into detail, and consequently from rendering this work as practically useful as I had hoped, it may not be altogether without benefit to expose, to the public eye, the atrocities which to this day are in full operation in that land of misery, and to point out the source from which, as I believe, a remedy can alone be hoped for.

The principles of my suggestions are comprised in the following propositions:—

1. That the present staple export of Africa renders to her inhabitants, at infinite cost, a miserable return of profit.

2. That the cultivation of her soil, and the barter of its productions, would yield an abundant harvest, and a copious supply of those articles which Africa requires.

3. That it is practicable to convince the African, experimentally, of the truth of these propositions, and thus to make him our confederate in the suppression of the Slave Trade.

I despair of being able to put down a traffic in which a vast continent is engaged, by the few ships we can afford to employ : as auxiliaries they are of great value, but alone they are insufficient. I do not dream of attempting to persuade the African, by appealing merely to his reason or his conscience, to renounce gainful guilt, and to forego those inhuman pursuits which gratify his cupidity, and supply his wants. But when the appeal we make is to his interest, and when his passions are enlisted on our side, there is nothing chimerical in the hope that he may be brought to exchange slender profits, with danger, for abundant gain, with security and peace.

If these views can be carried into effect, they have at least thus much to recommend them.

They will not plunge the country into hostility with any portion of the civilised world, for they involve no violation of international law. We may cultivate intercourse and innocent commerce with the natives of Africa, without abridging the rights or damaging the honest interests of any rival power.

They require no monopoly of trade ; if other nations choose to send their merchantmen to carry on legitimate traffic in Africa, they will but advance our object, and lend their aid in extinguishing that which we are resolved to put down.

They involve no schemes of conquest ; our ambition is of another order. Africa is now torn to pieces. She is the victim of the most iron despotism that the world ever saw: inveterate cruelty reigns over her broad territory. We desire to usurp nothing,—and to conquer nothing,—but the Slave Trade.

Finally, we ask of the Government only that which subjects have a right to expect from their rulers, namely, *protection to person and property* in their lawful pursuits.

Here I must pause; for I feel bound to confess, much as it may tend to shake the whole fabric of my views, that there is a great danger to which we shall be exposed, unless it be most carefully guarded against at the outset: the discovery of the fact that man as a labourer on the soil is superior in value to man as an article of merchandise may induce the continuance, if not the increase, of that internal slavery which now exists in Africa.

I hope we shall never be so deluded as to give the slightest toleration to anything like constrained labour. We must not put down one iniquity by abetting another. I believe implicitly that free labour will beat all other labour; that slavery, besides being a great crime, is a gross blunder; and that the most refined and sagacious policy we can pursue is, common honesty and undeviating justice. Let it then be held as a most sacred principle that, wherever our authority prevails, slavery shall cease; and that whatever influence we may obtain shall be employed in the same direction.

I have thus noticed several of the negative advantages which attach to these views, and I have frankly stated the danger which, as I conceive, attends them. I shall now briefly allude to one point, which, I own, weighs with me beyond all the other considerations, mighty as they are, which this great question involves.

Grievous, and this almost beyond expression, as are the physical evils endured by Africa, there is yet a more lamentable feature in her present condition. Bound in the chains of the grossest ignorance, she is a prey to the most savage superstition. Christianity has made but feeble inroads on this kingdom of darkness, nor can she hope to gain an entrance where the traffic in man pre-occupies the ground. But were this obstacle removed, Africa would present the finest field for the labours of Christian missionaries which the world has yet seen opened to them. I have no hesitation in stating my belief that there is in the negro race a capacity for receiving the truths of the Gospel beyond most other heathen nations; while, on the other hand, there is this remarkable, if not unique, circumstance in their case—that a race of teachers of their own blood is already in course of rapid preparation for them; that the providence of God has overruled even slavery and the Slave Trade for this end; and that from among the settlers of Sierra Leone, the peasantry of the West Indies, and the thousands of their children, now receiving Christian education, may be expected to arise a body of men who will return to the land of their fathers, carrying Divine truth and all its concomitant blessings into the heart of Africa.

One noble sacrifice in behalf of the negro race has already been made. In the words of the most eloquent citizen of another nation—" Great Britain, loaded with an unprecedented debt, and with a grinding taxation, contracted a new debt of a hundred million dollars, to give freedom, not to Englishmen, but to the degraded African. I know not that history records an act so disinterested, so sublime. In the progress of ages England's naval triumphs will shrink into a more and more narrow space in the records of our race. This moral triumph will fill a broader, brighter page." *

Another, it may be a more inveterate evil, remains,

* Dr. Channing.

—an evil which for magnitude and malignity stands without a parallel. One thousand human victims * (if my facts will bear sifting) are daily required to feed this vast and devouring consumer of mankind. In vain has Nature given to Africa noble rivers; man is the only merchandise they carry. In vain a fertile land;—lavish in wild and spontaneous productions, no cultivating hand calls forth its riches. In vain has she placed it in the vicinity of Civilisation and Christianity; within a few weeks' voyage of the Thames there is a people who worship the shark and the snake, and a prince who imagines the agency of an evil spirit in the common properties of the loadstone.† Africa is indeed encircled by an effectual barrier against the entrance of commerce, cultivation, and Christianity. That barrier is the Slave Trade.

It may be thought wild extravagance to indulge the hope that evils so rank are capable of cure. I do not deny that it is, of all tasks, the most arduous, or that it will require the whole energy of Great Britain; but if it shall be made a capital object of British policy, for the accomplishment of which our whole strength, if necessary, shall be put forward, and if it shall be, as I am sure it is, a cause in which we may look for Divine countenance and help, I see no reason for despair. What has been done,

---

* See page 170.   † Laird, vol. i. p. 219.

may be done again; and it is matter of history, that from superstitions as bloody, from a state of intellect as rude, and from the Slave Trade itself, a nation has been reclaimed, and now enjoys, in comparison with Africa, a blaze of light, liberty, religion, and happiness. That nation is Great Britain. What we find the African, the Romans found us;* and it is not unreasonable to hope that, in the language of Mr. Pitt, " even Africa will enjoy, at length, in the evening of her days, those blessings which have de-

---

* By the concurrent testimony of the best ancient historians, our forefathers were nothing better than "painted savages," the votaries of a sanguinary superstition which consumed its hecatombs of human victims ; " Alii immani magnitudine simulacra habent; quorum contexta viminibus membra vivis hominibus complent; quibus succensis, circumventi flammâ exanimantur homines." (Cæsar, Bell. Gall., l. vi. c. 16.) And, if we may credit the testimony of Diodorus Siculus, they were also addicted to cannibalism ; " for," says he, " the Gauls are such savages that they devour human flesh ; as do also those British nations which inhabit Ireland." (l. v. c. 32.) Cicero, in one of his letters, speaking of the success of an expedition against Britain, says, the only plunder to be found, consisted, " ex mancipiis; ex quibus nullos puto te literis aut musicis eruditos expectare;" thus, in the same sentence, proving the existence of the Slave Trade, and intimating that it was impossible that any Briton should be intelligent enough to be worthy to serve the accomplished Atticus. Ad Att. l. iv. 16. Henry, in his History of England, gives us also the authority of Strabo for the prevalence of the Slave Trade amongst us, and tells us that slaves were once an established article of our exports. " Great numbers," says he, " were exported from Britain, and were to be seen exposed for sale, like cattle, in the Roman market."—Henry, vol. ii. p. 225.

scended so plentifully upon us in a much earlier period of the world."

To raise Africa from the dust is an object worthy of the efforts of the highest order of ambition. It is calculated that Napoleon, in the course of his career, occasioned the sacrifice of three millions of the human race. The suppression of the Slave Trade would, in a very few years, save as many lives as he was permitted to destroy. The most patriotic and loyal amongst us cannot frame a loftier wish for our country and its sovereign, than that her reign, which, in its dawn, witnessed the deliverance of our colonies from slavery, may be prolonged, till, through British agency, Africa shall also be released from a still greater curse:—not, however, for the honour's sake, though it would give imperishable renown; nor for the profit's sake, though it promises to open boundless fields for capital, industry and enterprise; but in pity to Africa, and for His favour who has said—" Undo the heavy burdens, let the oppressed go free, and break every yoke." " Then shall thy light break forth as the morning ;" " and the glory of the Lord shall be thy rereward."*

* Isaiah lviii. 6, 8.

THE SLAVE TRADE.

" You will perceive that this horrid traffic has been carried on to an extent that almost staggers belief."

Commodore Sir Robert Mends, Sierra Leone.

In preparing this work, my chief purpose has been to offer some views which I entertain of the most effectual mode of suppressing the Slave Trade; but before I enter upon these, I must state the extent to which that traffic is now carried on, and the sacrifice of human life which it occasions.

EXTENT.

My *first* proposition is, that upwards of 150,000 human beings are annually conveyed from Africa, across the Atlantic, and sold as slaves.

It is almost impossible to arrive at the exact extent to which any contraband trade, much more a trade so revolting, is carried on. It is the interest of those concerned in it to conceal all evidence of their guilt; and the Governor of a Portuguese colony is not very likely, at once to connive at the crime, and to confess that it is extensively practised. By the mode of calculation I propose to adopt, it is very possible I may err; but the error must be on the

B

right side; I may underrate, it is almost impossible that I can exaggerate, the extent of the traffic. With every disposition on the part of those who are engaged in it to veil the truth, certain facts have, from time to time, transpired, sufficient to show, if not the full amount of the evil, at least, that it is one of prodigious magnitude.

I commence with what appears to be the most considerable slave market, viz.—that of

BRAZIL.

In the papers on the subject of the Slave Trade annually presented to Parliament, by authority of his Majesty (and entitled, "Class A" and "Class B"), the following official information is given by the British Vice-Consul at Rio de Janeiro, as to the number of slaves imported there :—

From 1 July to 31 Dec. 1827	15,481[1]
From 1 Jan. to 31 March, 1828 . . .	15,483[2]
From 1 April to 30 June, 1828, say . .	11,532[3]
From 1 July to 31 Dec. 1828	24,488[4]
From 1 Jan. to 30 June, 1829	25,179[5]
From 1 July to 31 Dec. 1829	22,813[6]
From 1 Jan. to 30 June, 1830	33,964[7]
	———
	148,940

[1] Class B, 1828, p. 105.   [2] Class B, 1828, p. 107.

[3] No returns. These numbers are given on the average of the three months previous to, and three months subsequent to the dates here mentioned.

[4] Class B, 1829, pp. 80, 81.   [5] Class B, 1829, p. 89.

[6] Ditto, 1830, p. 71.   [7] Ditto, 1830, p. 78.

That is, in the twelve months

preceding the 30th June,	1828	.	.	.	42,964
„	„	1829	.	. .	49,667
„	„	1830	.	. .	56,777

148,940

Thus it stands confessed, upon authority which cannot be disputed, that from the 1st of July, 1827, to the 30th of June, 1830 (three years), there were brought into the single port of Rio de Janeiro, 148,940 negroes, or, on an average, 49,643 annually. It appears also, that, in the last year, the number was swelled to 56,777 per annum.*

Caldcleugh, in his Travels in South America, speaking of the Slave Trade at Rio, (which, however, was not then so extensive as it now is,) states, " that there are *three* other ports in Brazil trading *to the same extent.*"† If this be correct, the number of negroes annually imported vastly exceeds any estimate I have formed; but it is more safe to rely on the authority of the British Commissioners,‡ scanty as

---

* I see in the *Patriot* newspaper of 25th June last (1838), the following statement :—" A Brazil mail has brought advices from Rio to the 22nd April. That fine country appears to be making rapid strides in civilisation and improvement; the only drawback is the inveterate and continued encouragement of the slave-trade. The Rover corvette had just captured two slavers, having 494 negroes on board ; and the traffic is said to amount to 60,000 annually, into Rio alone, almost entirely carried on under Portuguese colours.

† Caldcleugh's Travels, London, 1825, vol. ii. p. 56.

‡ By the treaties with foreign powers for the suppression of the Slave Trade, Commissioners are appointed to act as Judges, in a

it necessarily is. They reside in the capital; and their distance from the three outports of itself might render it difficult for them to obtain full information. But when to the distance is added the still greater difficulty arising from the anxiety on the part of almost all the Brazilian functionaries to suppress information on the subject, it is clearly to be inferred that the number stated by the Commissioners must fall materially below the truth. They tell us, however, that in a year and a-half, from 1st of January, 1829, to 30th of June, 1830, the numbers imported were, into

Bahia	22,202
Pernambuco	8,079
Maranham	1,252
	31,533
To these we must also add those imported into the port of Para .	799
Total in eighteen months . .	32,332*
Or annually	21,554
To which add Rio, as before stated†	56,777
And we have for the annual number landed in Brazil . . .	78,331

So many, *at least*, were landed. That number is undisputed. The amount, however, great as it is,

Court of Mixed Commission for the adjudication of captured slave-vessels.

* Class B, 1829, 1830.   † P. 3.

probably falls short of the reality. If the question were put to me, what is the number which I believe to be annually landed in Brazil? I should rate it considerably higher. I conceive that the truth lies between the maximum as taken from Caldcleugh, and the minimum as stated in the Official Returns; and I should conjecture that the real amount would be moderately rated at 100,000, brought annually into these five Brazilian ports. But as the question is, not how many I suppose, but how many I can show, to be landed, I must confine myself to what I can prove; and I have proved that 78,331 were landed at five ports in Brazil, in the course of twelve months, ending at the 30th June, 1830.

But is it easy to believe, while Brazil receives so vast a number into five of her principal ports, that the trade is confined to them, and that none are introduced along the remaining line of her coast, extending over 38 degrees of latitude, or about 2,600 miles, and abounding in harbours, rivers, and creeks, where disembarkation can easily be effected?

It may safely be assumed, that the slave-trader would desire to avoid notoriety, and to escape the duty which is paid upon all imports; either of these motives may induce him to smuggle his negroes ashore. That numbers are so smuggled, is established by the fact, that most vessels from the coast of Africa report themselves in ballast on arriving at Bahia. In the last Parliamentary Papers,* more than half the vessels are found to have reported

* Class B, 1837, and Class B, Farther Series, 1837.

themselves in ballast, and the remainder to have come from Prince's Island, Ajuda (Wydah), and Angola, —the very places where the Slave Trade most prevails.* The Commissioners interpret these returns in ballast thus:—" In the six months ending 30th June, 1836, twenty vessels entered this port (Rio) from the coast of Africa; they came in ballast, and, upon the usual declaration, that the master or pilot had died on the voyage, were stopped, with scarcely an exception, by the police, on suspicion of having landed slaves on the coast; but as usual also, were; after a few days detention, released."† The Juiz di Direito, of Ilha Grande, (one of the few functionaries who appears to have done his duty with respect to the Slave Trade, and whose activity has been rewarded, on the part of the populace, by attempts on his life, and on the part of the Brazilian Government, as I have been informed, by dismissal from his office,) confirms this view of the Commissioners in a Report, dated 12th November, 1834, in which he says :—" I see that in the trade in Africans brought to this district are committed almost the whole population of this place, and of the neighbouring district." " Here, since I have been in the district, there have been twenty-two disembarkations, which I can remember; and I can assure your Excellency, that an equal, or even a greater number have called off this port; and it is certain that they did not return to Africa."‡

* Class B, 1837, p. 83.   † Class A, 1836, p. 251.
‡ Class B, 1834, p. 233.

It is then clear that, over and above the number annually introduced into the five ports, negroes are landed along the line of the Brazilian coast; but as we have no facts to guide us to the precise number, I will assume that the trading in slaves is confined to these five places, and that not a single negro was landed in Brazil beyond the 78,331 negroes in twelve months, ending in June, 1830.

I admit that this proves little, as to the Slave Trade at the present time. It is very possible that it raged at a former period, but that it has now ceased; and it may be argued that the facts stated were prior to the treaty with Great Britain, and that the operation of that treaty has considerably reduced the number. If we are to believe the official reports made to our Government, it is just the reverse. The Slave Trade has increased since that time. The Brazilian Minister of Marine recommends to his government the formation of a " *cordon sanitaire,* which may prevent the access to our shores of those swarms of Africans that are continually poured forth from vessels engaged in so abominable a traffic."* This, be it observed, was on the 17th of June, 1833, three years after the treaty had come into operation.

The Ministers of Foreign Affairs and of Justice, in their report of the Chamber of Deputies, in 1835, speak " of the continuance of the traffic, to an extent at once frightful to humanity, and alarming to the best interests of the country." " The fury

* Class A, 1833, p. 58.

of this barbarous traffic continues every day to increase with a constantly progressing force."   " Sixteen hundred new blacks are openly maintained on
an estate in the neighbourhood of Ilha Grande."
" The continued—we might almost say the uninterrupted—traffic in slaves is carrying on, on these
coasts."[1] On the 17th June, 1836, Mr. Gore Ouseley,
British resident at Rio Janeiro, states in his despatch, that " The Slave Trade is carried on in Brazil
with more activity than ever[2]." In the preceding
May, in a despatch to Viscount Palmerston, he
speaks of " an association of respectable persons who
were going to use steam-boats for the importation of
Africans[3]."

In March, 1836, the President of Bahia observed,
in a speech to the Assembly of that province, "That
the contraband in slaves continues with the same
scandal[4]." In the following September the British
Commissioners say, " At no period, perhaps, has the
trade been ever carried on with more activity or
daring[5]." And again, in November, 1836, " The
traffic in slaves is every day becoming more active
and notorious on this coast."

Thus, then, not only by the reports of our Commissioners and our Resident, but by the admission of
the Brazilians themselves, it appears, that the Save
Trade has increased since the treaty was formed.

[1] Class A, 1835, p. 265.   [2] Class B, 1836, p. 63.
[3] Class B, 1836, p. 67.   [4] Class A, 1836, p. 231.
[5] Class A, 1836, p. 250.   [6] Class A, 1836, p. 260.

It seems hardly necessary to add, that I have received letters to the same effect from gentlemen on whom I have entire reliance. A naval officer, in a letter dated 16th September, 1835, says, " For the last six months the importation of new slaves is greater than ever remembered." A gentleman writes to me, of date 7th April, 1837, " It may be well to acquaint you, that the Slave Trade has now got to an unprecedented pitch."

The Parliamentary Papers presented in 1838, remarkably confirm the two positions which I have laid down; first, that the Slave Trade is enormous; and, secondly, that so far from abating, it has increased since the period when the treaty was formed.

By a private letter from a highly respectable quarter, I learn that in the month of December, 1836, the importation of slaves into the province of Rio alone was not less than   . .   4,831

Our Minister at Rio states that there

arrived in the following month of

January, 1837	4,870[1]
February	1,992[2]
March	7,395[3]
April	5,596[4]
May	2,753[5]

                                        27,437

[1] Class B, 1837, p. 58.
[2] Ibid. —— 60.
[3] Ibid. —— 64.
[4] Class B, 1837, p. 65.
[5] Ibid. ——— 71.

Thus, within six months, in the province of Rio, or the vicinity, there were known to have been landed this vast number. This is hardly disputed by the Brazilian authorities. Our Minister at Rio, in a letter to Lord Palmerston, dated 18th April, 1837, speaking of 7,395 negroes landed in the preceding month, says:—"As a satisfactory proof of the general accuracy of these reports, it may be observed here, that the Government has excepted to two only of the numerous items they comprehend."*

It would be an error to suppose that these reported numbers comprehend anything like the whole amount of the importations: conclusive evidence to the contrary appears in a variety of passages of the same reports. I shall take but one as an instance. Mr. Hamilton, in his Enclosure of 1st March, 1837, states as follows:—"Brig *Johovah* from Angola. This vessel, since she left this port, thirteen months ago, has made three voyages without entering any port. The first voyage she landed 700 slaves, very sickly, at Ponta Negra, about half way betwixt this port and Cape Frio; on the second voyage, 600 slaves at the island of St. Sebastian; and on the present voyage, 520 slaves at Tapier, close to the entrance of this port. The greater number of these last were put into boats and fishing canoes, and brought to town."† The last number, namely 520, only, are reported in the return for the month of February preceding; but the remaining 1300 have

* Class B, 1837, p. 63.   † Class B, 1837, p. 60.

not appeared in any returns. It is evident from this, as well as many other passages, that vessels land their negroes on the coast, and return direct to Africa, and all who do so, escape notice, and are not included in the account. If these 1300 are added to the returns for the first six months in the year 1837, the importations into Rio alone for this year will exceed those of 1830.

So much for the province of Rio. I would next observe as to Pernambuco. In a letter from Mr. Watts, the British Consul, to Lord Palmerston, of date 5th May, 1837, he says, " I have just received directions to furnish Mr. Hamilton with a monthly return of vessels arriving from the coast of Africa, at any port within my consulate," &c. ; and he adds, " the supineness, not to say connivance, of the Government of Brazil in general on the subject in reference, the gross venality of subordinate officers, the increasing demand of hands for the purposes of husbandry, the enormous profits derivable from this inhuman traffic, which is rapidly increasing at this port in the most undisguised manner, combined with the almost insuperable difficulty of procuring authentic information through private channels *from the dread of the assassin's knife or bullet, even in the* OPEN *day, and in the public gaze ;* and the dark and artful combinations of the dealers in slaves, their agents, and the agriculturists, to mask and facilitate the disembarkation of imported slaves ;—all these glaring and obstructive facts combine to render the attainment of authentic data on which to ground effective official representation on the subject of the unprecedented increase of the Slave Trade all along the coast of Brazil, an almost insurmountable obstacle."*

The case then may be stated thus : prior to the treaty the annual importation of negroes into *five* ports of Brazil was 78,333, to which might be added the indefinite but considerable number smuggled into other places in Brazil. Since that time the trade has, by general testimony, increased. Notwithstanding the difficulty thrown in the way of obtaining information, the facts which we have been enabled to glean, demonstrate what the Marquis of Barbacena stated in the Senate of Brazil on the 30th June, 1837, namely, " *That it may be safely asserted, without fear of exaggeration, that during the last three years, the importation has been much more considerable, than it had ever before been when the commerce was unfettered and legal.*" † On these grounds we might be entitled to make a considerable addition. It is enough for us to know, that at the *very least*, 78,333 human beings are annually torn from Africa, and are imported into Brazil.

Cuba.

It is scarcely practicable to ascertain the number of slaves imported into Cuba : it can only

* Class B, 1837, p. 84.   † Class B, 1837, p. 69.

be a calculation on, at best, doubtful data. We are continually told by the Commissioners, that difficulties are thrown in the way of obtaining correct information in regard to the Slave Trade in that island. Everything that artifice, violence, intimidation, popular countenance, and official connivance can do, is done, to conceal the extent of the traffic. Our ambassador, Mr. Villiers, April, 1837, says, "That a privilege (that of entering the harbour after dark), denied to all other vessels, is granted to the slave-trader; and, in short, that with the servants of the Government, the misconduct of the persons concerned in this trade finds favour and protection. The crews of captured vessels are permitted to purchase their liberation; and it would seem that the persons concerned in this trade have resolved upon setting the Government of the mother country at defiance."* Almost the only specific fact which I can collect from the reports of the Commissioners, is the statement, "that 1835 presents a number of slave vessels (arriving at the Havana), by which there must have been landed, at the very least, 15,000 negroes."† But in an official letter, dated 28th May, 1836, there is the following remarkable passage:— " I wish I could add, that this list contains even one-fourth of the number of those which have entered after having landed cargoes, or sailed after having refitted in this harbour‡." This would give an

* Class B, 1837, p. 2.   † Class A, 1335, p. 206.
‡ Class A, 1836, p. 153.

amount of 60,000 for the Havana alone; but is
Havana the only port in Cuba in which negroes
are landed? The reverse is notoriously true. The
Commissioner says, "I have every reason to believe
that several of the other ports of Cuba, more particularly the distant city of St. Jago de Cuba, carry
on the traffic to a considerable extent." Indeed,
it is stated by Mr. Hardy, the consul at St.
Jago, in a letter to Lord Palmerston, of the 18th
February, 1837, "That the Portuguese brig *Boca
Negra* landed on the 6th instant at Juragua, a little
to windward of this port (St. Jago), 400 Africans of
all ages, and subsequently entered this port."* But
in order that we may be assuredly within the mark,
no claim shall be made on account of these distant
ports. Confining ourselves to the Havana, it would
seem probable, if it be not demonstrated, that the
number for that port, *a fortiori*, for the whole island,
may fairly be estimated at 60,000.† I have many
strong grounds for believing that this is no exaggeration, one of which I will name. At a meeting

---

* Class B, 1837, p. 29.

† THE SLAVE TRADE.—" It has occurred to us, now that
the Spaniards and Portuguese are pushing the inhuman traffic
with so much zeal and energy, whether it would not be preferable
to employ steamers than sailing-vessels in cruising about that grand
receptacle of stolen Africans, the island of Cuba. *We have heard
it stated that upwards of sixty vessels per month arrive in Cuba
from the coast of Africa with slaves.* Supposing that each vessel
on an average carries two hundred of these, and that the number
of arrivals continue the same for one year certain, we should have

which I had with several merchants and captains of vessels trading to the coast of Africa, I inquired what was the proportion of the slave trade with Cuba compared with that of Brazil? Captain M'Lean, governor of Cape Coast Castle (than whom no one has better opportunities of information, as all the vessels from the Bight of Benin, in their way to St. Thomas, pass his fort), stated that, as far as he could judge, there were three for Cuba, to two for Brazil, and in this opinion every person present on the occasion concurred.*

Having proved that there are landed in Brazil at least 78,000, this would give to Cuba more than 100,000. But let the minor number be taken as deduced from the reports of the Commissioners, and the account will stand thus :—

the incredible number of one hundred and forty-four thousand slaves imported into that colony in twelve months! Although we cannot believe that the trade is carried on to this extent, still we think the Government is called upon to resort to prompt and vigorous measures to repress, if not put a stop to it. Whether steamers would be preferable to schooners, such as were previously employed, we are not seamen enough to decide; certainly the slavers would have less chance of escape from the former than the latter."—*Watchman, February* 21, 1838.

* Since the above went to press, I have learnt on good authority, " that there have been about 100,000 boxes of sugar, of 400lbs. each, exported from Cuba during the season just closed (July, 1838), more than in any preceding;" and that a very intelligent merchant in that island had declared, " that he knew of no fewer than forty new estates that had been lately opened, remembering that it will take about two years to make them productive."

Cuba 60,000
Brazil 78,333
_____
138,333

To this number of slaves actually landed
must be added those who have been
captured, which on the average of
the years 1836 and 1837, was at
Sierra Leone 7,852
_____
146,185

And at Havana in 1837 . . 442
_____

I cannot find that any have been ad-
judicated at Rio.

Further than this I cannot go by actual
proof; but there can be no doubt, that
the Slave Trade has other victims than
those included in this table. For example,
we know that several slave vessels are
annually wrecked or founder at sea;*
though it is impossible to arrive at anything like exact numbers. Many negroes
also are thrown overboard, either during
a chase, or from dearth of provisions and
water.†

For these, I will assume 3,373
_____

Total. . 150,000

* See Wrecks, &c., page 139, &c.
† See p. 130, Captain Wauchope, R.N. See also the Paris
Petition at p. 118.

I have no authority for this assumption of 3373, it is merely a guess ; it may be excessive. I only take this number to make a round sum. And if in this trivial point I have gone beyond the mark, I shall give abundant compensation for it hereafter.

I will next take the case of the Island of

PORTO RICO.

In regard to Porto Rico, I learn, from the valuable work of Colonel Flinter, entitled ' Present State of the Island of Porto Rico,' some important facts ; the exports from that island were—

In 1814 . . . 500,840 dollars.
1830 . . 3,411,845

The amount of sugar produced has increased
from 37,969 arrobas in 1810
to 414,663 ,, in 1830

He calculates that there are only 45,000 slaves in the island; but he tells us that the landed proprietors conceal the real number of their slaves in order to escape a tax.

From the Parliamentary Papers of 1837, it appears, as stated by Mr. Courtenay, the British Consul at Port-au-Prince, Haiti, " that a slaving schooner, under the Brazilian flag, called Pacquette de Capo Verde, was wrecked on the Folle reefs near Aux Cayes, on the 28th February, 1837, having previously landed his cargo at Ponce, in the Island of Porto Rico."* It appears, also, that one-ninth

* Class B, 1837, p. 140.

C

part of all the vessels condemned at Sierra Leone in 1837 were bound for Porto Rico, and that one of them, at least, the Descubierta, belonged to the island and was built there.*

In a Report by the Commissioners at Sierra Leone, of date 20th March, 1837, it is stated that the Temerario had been captured with 352 slaves on board, bound for the Island of Port Rico; † the Commissioners, on the 25th of April following, report the case of the Cinco Amigos, "belonging to the Spanish Island of Porto Rico, where slaving adventures have latterly been fitted out, with increased activity." ‡

A gentleman, on whom I can rely, has informed me that in November, 1836, he saw two slave-vessels fitting out in the harbour of Porto Rico, and on his return in March, 1837, he saw a slaver entering the harbour, and he learned on the spot from good authority that about 7000 negroes had been landed in the space of the preceding year.

From the above facts, especially from the increased production of sugar ; from the constant smuggling communication which is known to exist with the slave-mart of St. Thomas ; from the circumstance that apprentices have been kidnapped by their masters in the British settlement of Anguilla, § for the purpose of being carried to Porto

---

* Class A, (Farther Series), 1837, pp. 5, 13.

† Class A, 1837, p. 50.　　‡ Class A, 1837, p. 28.

§ Class B, 1837, p. 10.

Rico,—and from the fact, that there is some Slave Trade with that island, it is not difficult to come to the conclusion, that there has been a traffic in slaves to a considerable amount. Upon the same principle, however, which has led me to wave all additions to which any shade of doubt may attach, I will not claim any increase on the sum of slaves exported from Africa in respect of Porto Rico.

BUENOS AYRES, ETC.

I am afraid that some addition might too justly be claimed with regard to Buenos Ayres, Rio de la Plata, and the United Provinces of the Uruguay.

In a letter from Mr. Hood to Lord Palmerston, dated from Buenos Ayres, 1833, it is stated, " that the dormant spirit of Slave Trading has been awakened ;" that " the Aguila Primera, a schooner belonging to this place, and under this flag, was fitting, and in a forward state, to proceed to the coast of Congo for a cargo of slaves ; and that other fast-sailing vessels were in request for the same service." The Uruguese minister did not deny that the Government were cognisant of the proceedings, and confessed that " they had given their concurrence to import 2000 colonists from the coast of Africa, which he considered a fair and legitimate trade." Nor is it to be wondered at, that he had arrived at so extraordinary a conclusion; for it appears by the same letter that the same " minister had received a bribe of 30,000 dollars to permit a

company of merchants to import 2000 slaves, under
the denomination of colonists."*

In September, 1834, Lord Palmerston, in a letter
to Mr. Hamilton, states that "the Slave Trade is
now increasing in the River Plata, supported by the
capital of Monte Video citizens, and covered by the
flag of the United Provinces of the Uruguay," and
that the Abolition Law is wholly without effect.†

How unavailing were the remonstrances then
made, appears by the fact of the seizure, on the
10th November, 1834, of the Rio da Prata, a slave-
brig of 202 tons, under the flag of Monte Video,
with licence from the authorities to import 650 colonists, with 521 slaves on board, men, women, and
children."‡

"We may form some idea," says Mr. M'Queen,
"of the numbers imported into the Argentine Republic, from the fact that, in 1835 (see Porter's
Tables), twenty Portuguese vessels departed for
Africa, and as many arrived from it in the port of
Monte Video, after landing their cargoes of slaves
from Africa on the adjacent coasts."

It is most disheartening to find, that, in spite of
all our efforts, the Slave Trade, instead of ceasing
where it has long prevailed, is spreading over these
new and petty states; and that the first use they
make of their flag (which but for us they never
would have possessed) is to thwart Great Britain,

* Class B, 1833, pp. 55 and 56.   † Class B, 1834, p. 81.
‡ Class B, 1835, p. 141.

and to cover the Slave Trade; and, farther, to learn that their slave-traffic is attended with even more than the usual horrors. It must not be forgotten that, as we have just seen, for a voyage from the southern coast of Africa to Monte Video, (a voyage of some thousands of miles,) the space allowed is less than one ton for three slaves.

Lists are given in the Parliamentary Papers of many vessels employed in the Slave Trade, which are continually arriving at, or sailing from, Monte Video;* but it seems hardly necessary to pursue the subject further. We know there is a Slave Trade with these states; but as we have no data to compute the extent of it, I cannot avail myself of the fact, however certain it may be. I must, therefore, in regard to these countries, as I have done in the case of Porto Rico, wave extending my calculations. I will next advert to

THE UNITED STATES.

In the Report of the Commissioners at Havana, for 1836, dated 25th Oct. 1836, I find these words :—" During the months of August and September (1836) there arrived here for sale, from the United States, several new schooners, some of which were already expressly fitted for the Slave Trade.

" The Emanuel and Dolores were purchased, and have since left the port (we believe with other names) on slaving expeditions, under the Spanish flag."

* Class B, 1835, pp. 141—143.

II " But to our astonishment and regret, we have ascertained that the Anaconda and Viper, the one on the 6th, and the other on the 10th, current, cleared out and sailed from hence, for the Cape de Verde Islands, under the American flag.

" These two vessels *arrived in the Havana, fitted in every particular for the Slave Trade;* and took on board a cargo which would at once have condemned, *as a slaver,* any vessel belonging to the nations that are parties to the equipment article."*

The Commissioners farther observe, that the declaration of the American President " not to make the United States a party to any convention on the subject of the Slave Trade, has been the means of inducing American citizens to build and fit, in their own ports, vessels, only calculated for piracy or the Slave Trade, to enter this harbour, and, in concert with the Havana slave-traders, to take on board a prohibited cargo, manacles, &c. ; and proceed openly to that notorious depôt for this iniquitous traffic, the Cape de Verde Islands, under the shelter of their national flag :" and "we may add, that, while these American slavers were making their final arrangements for departure, the Havana was visited more than once by American ships of war, as well as British and French."

The Commissioners also state, that " two American vessels, the Fanny Butler and Rosanna,

* Class A, 1836, p. 191.

have proceeded to the Cape de Verde Islands, and the coast of Africa, under the American flag, upon the same inhuman speculation."* A few months afterwards they report that—" We cannot conceal our deep regret at the *new and dreadful impetus* imparted to the Slave Trade of this island (Cuba), by the manner in which some American citizens impunibly violate every law, by embarking openly for the coast of Africa under their national flag, with the avowed purpose of bringing slaves to this market.† We are likewise assured that it is intended, by means of this flag, to supply slaves for the vast province of Texas; agents from thence being in constant communication with the Havana Slave Merchants."‡

This "new and dreadful impetus" to the Slave Trade, predicted by our commissioners, has already come to pass. In a list of the departure of vessels for the coast of Africa, from the Havana, up to a recent date, I find that, "in the last four months," no other flags than those of Portugal and the United States have been used to cover slavers.§

---

* Class A, 1836, pp. 191, 192.

† Class A, 1836, p. 218, and Class B, 1836, pp. 123 and 129.

‡ While preparing this work for the press, I received a communication from Major M'Gregor, late Special Magistrate at the Bahamas, in which he notices the wreck of the schooner Invincible, on the 28th October 1837, on one of these islands; and he adds, " the captain's name was Potts, a native of Florida. The vessel was fitted out at Baltimore in America, and three-fourths of the crew were natives of the United States, although they pretended to be only passengers."

§ The Venus, said to be the sharpest clipper built vessel ever constructed at Baltimore, left that place in July 1838, and arrived at

The list states that vessels, fitted for the Slave Trade, sailed from Havana for the coast of Africa, bearing the American flag, as follows :—

		American.
During the month of June, 1838,	2
,,	July,	2
,,	August	5
,,	September	1
		10

No symptom in the case is so alarming as this. It remains to be seen, whether America will endure that her flag shall be the refuge of these dealers in human blood.

I confidently hope better things for the peace of Africa and for the honour of the United States.

This leads me to the province of

TEXAS.

I have been informed, upon high authority, that "within the last twelve months* 15,000 negroes

Havana on the 4th of August following. She sailed from thence, in September, for Mozambique; there she took in a cargo of slaves, being all this time under the flag of the United States. On the 7th January, 1839, she landed 860 negroes near Havana, under Portuguese colours; and on the 9th these blacks with 1200 more were seen at one of the Barracoons, within two miles of that city, " exposed for sale, and presenting a most humiliating and melancholy spectacle."—PRIVATE LETTERS.

* Referring to 1837 and 1838.

were imported from Africa into Texas." I have the
greatest reliance on the veracity of the gentleman
from whom this intelligence comes; but I would
fain hope that he is in error. I can conceive no
calamity to Africa greater than that Texas should
be added to the number of the slave-trading states.
It is a gulf which will absorb millions of the human
race. I have proof, quite independent of any statements in this work, that not less than four millions
of negroes have in the last half-century been torn
from Africa for the supply of Brazil. Texas, once
polluted with the Slave Trade, will require a number
still more appalling.

In the case of Texas, as I have not sufficient
proof to adduce in support of the numbers which it
is reported have been carried into that country,
I shall, as I have already done in similar instances,
wave my claim for increasing my general estimate.

SUMMARY.

I have then brought the case to this point. There
is Slave Trading, although to an unknown and indefinite amount, into Porto Rico; into Texas; and
into some of the South American republics.

There is the strongest presumptive evidence, that
the Slave Trade into the five ports of Brazil which
have been noticed, is "much more considerable"
than my estimate makes it; and that I have also
underrated the importation of negroes into Cuba.
There are even grounds for suspicion that there are

other places (besides Porto Rico, Texas, Cuba, Monte Video, &c., and Brazil), where slaves are introduced; but for all these presumptions I reckon nothing, I take no account of them; I limit myself to the facts which I have established, viz., that there are, at the present time, imported annually

into Brazil	78,333
That the annual importations into Cuba amount to	60,000
That there have been captured . .	8,294
And I assume that the casualties* amount to	3,373

Making together   150,000

Corroborative Proofs of the Extent of the Slave Trade.

I confess there is something startling in the assertion, that so vast a number are annually carried from Africa to various parts of the New World.

Such a statement may well be received with some degree of doubt, and even suspicion. I have not been wholly free from these feelings myself, and I have again and again gone over the public documents, on which I have alone relied, in order to detect any inaccuracy which might lurk in them, or in the inferences deduced from them. No such mistake can I discover; but my conviction that the calculation is not excessive, has been fortified by finding that other persons, who have had access to

* See pp. 130, 139, &c.

other sources of information, and who rest their estimates on other data than those on which I have relied, make the number of human beings torn from Africa still greater than I do.

For example:—Captain M'Lean, Governor of Cape Coast Castle for many years, who estimates the extent of the Slave Trade by the vessels which he has seen passing along the coast, rates the number of slaves annually taken from the Bights of Benin and Biafra alone at 140,000.

In a letter from that gentleman, dated June 11, 1838, he says:—

Sir,

In compliance with your wishes, I beg leave to state to you, in this form, what I have already mentioned to you verbally; namely, that "in the year 1834, I have every reason to believe that the number of Slaves carried off from the Bights of Benin and Biafra amounted to 140,000." I have not beside me the *particular data* whereon I grounded this calculation; but I can state generally, that I founded it upon the number of slave-vessels which actually passed the forts on the Gold Coast during that year, and of those others, of whose presence on the coast I had certain information from her Majesty's cruisers or otherwise. When I say that I have rather under than over-stated the number, I ought at the same time to state that, in the years 1834—5, more slavers appeared on the coast than on any previous year within my observation; and this was partially, at least, accounted for (by those engaged in the traffic) by the fact of the cholera having swept off a large number of the slaves in the Island of Cuba. The ports of Bahia, also, were opened for the introduction of slaves, after having been shut for some time previous, on account of an insurrection among the negro population in that country.

This does not include the slaves embarked from the many notorious slave-ports to the northward of

Cape Coast, nor those carried from the eastern shores of Africa, nor those who are shipped at Loango, and the rest of the south-western coast. I confess that I have not any very clear grounds for calculating or estimating the numbers shipped from these three quarters. Along the south-eastern coast, we know that there are a great many ports from whence slaves are taken. With respect to the majority of these, we are left in the dark, as to the extent to which the Slave Trade is carried on; but in a few cases we have specific information. For example :—in the letters found on board the Soleil, which was captured by Commodore Owen, H.M.S. Leven, we have the following statement :—" From the port of Mozambique are exported every year upwards of 10,000 blacks."* Commodore Owen, in the account of his voyage to the eastern coast, informs us, that from eleven to fourteen slave-vessels come annually from Rio Janeiro to Quilimane and return with from 400 to 500 slaves each, on an average, which would amount to about 5500. †

Captain Cook‡ has informed me that, during the year 1837, 21 slave-vessels sailed from Mozambique, with an average cargo of 400 slaves each, making 8400. These, added to 7200 exported from Quilimane in eighteen vessels, also in 1837, according to Captain

* Class B, 1828, p. 84.

† Owen's Voyage, &c., London, 1833, vol. i. p. 293.

‡ Captain Cook commanded a trading vessel, employed on the East coast of Africa, in 1836, 7, and 8.

Cook, give a total of 15,600 slaves conveyed to Brazil and Cuba from these two ports alone. Of all the vessels, in number about thirty-eight, which sailed from the eastern coast in that year, Captain Cook believes that only one was captured. He adds,—" Some slaves are shipped from Inhambane, and other places along the coast;" but, having no accurate information, he has altogether omitted them.

Lieutenant Bosanquet, of H.M.S. Leveret, in a letter addressed to Admiral Sir P. Campbell, dated 29th September, 1837, says :—" From my observations last year, and from the information I have since been able to obtain, I conceive that upwards of 12,000 slaves must have left the east coast of Africa in 1836, for the Brazils and Cuba; and I think, from the number of vessels already arrived, * and there being many more expected, that that number will not be much decreased this year."†

We now turn to the south-western coast :—

In 1826 the Governor of Benguela informed Commodore Owen, that " Some years back that place had enjoyed greater trade than St. Paul de Loando, having then an annual averaged export of 20,000 slaves."‡ Owen also informs us that " From St. Paul de Loando 18,000 to 20,000 slaves are said to be annually exported, in great part to Brazil; but

* The letter is dated at the close of the rainy season on the eastern coast.

† Class B, Farther Series, 1837, p. 25.

‡ Owen's Voyage, &c., vol. ii. p. 272.

that the supply had considerably decreased on account of the dishonesty of the black agents in the country."

Commodore Owen shortly afterwards (in 1827) visited Kassenda, near the river Congo, which place, he says, "is principally resorted to by slavers, of whom five were at anchor, in the harbour, on our arrival, one French, and the rest under the Brazilian flag."*

On looking over the Slave Trade papers presented to Parliament in 1838,† I find it stated, in monthly lists, that in the course of the year 1837 seventy vessels were reported by the British authorities to have imported into the vicinity of Rio Janeiro 29,929 slaves, from Angola, Benguela, and Loando. All these vessels came in ballast to the port of Rio Janeiro, after having landed their slaves on the coast.

The reader will see, vide pp. 4, 5, that there are other points in Brazil at which slaves are disembarked. To say nothing of these, though the consul at one of them reports the arrival of the Portuguese brig Aleide, from Angola, on the 10th July, 1837, having previously landed 460 slaves in the neighbourhood; though the consul at another states that "the frequent disembarkation of negroes imported from the coast of Africa in the vicinities of this port, is the common public talk of the day;" and though the vice-consul at a third, notices the arrival of three

* Owen's Voyage, &c., vol. ii. 292.
† Class B, 1837, and Class B, Farther Series, 1837.

vessels from Angola in the months of November and December, 1836, I only claim from Angola 29,929 negroes landed in Brazil in 1837.

Then, as to the ports and rivers to the north of Cape Palmas, I find that General Turner, late Governor of Sierra Leone, in a despatch dated the 20th December, 1825, states that the exports of slaves from that part of the coast amounts annually to 30,000.*

From these extracts it appears that we have satisfactory evidence that the export of slaves from the south-eastern coast of Africa to America amounts annually to, say, ... 15,000
From Angola, &c. to America . . 29,929
From the ports to the northward of Cape
    Coast to America 30,000
                                     _____

        Amounting in all to . . . 74,929
Thus then stands the case. We have information that the Slave Trade prevails in a variety of ports and rivers besides those in the Bights of Benin and Biafra. This information, though conclusive as to the fact that the Slave Trade prevails, is vague as to the extent to which it is carried on; but we have specific authority to this extent, that from a limited number of these ports there is an annual draft of about 75,000
To these we must confine ourselves, and
these, added to 140,000

* Extracted from the Records of the Colonial Office for 1825.

given by Mr. M'Lean for the export
from the Bights of Benin and Biafra,
make the total annual Slave Trade   ———
between Africa and America amount to   215,000

If we deduct from this number the usual amount
of mortality, it will leave a remainder not very different from, though somewhat exceeding, the estimate of 150,000 landed annually in America.

With another gentleman, Mr. M'Queen, whose
authority I have already quoted, I did not become
acquainted till after the time that I had completed
my own estimate. His channels of information
are totally distinct from mine. Besides being conversant with all the information which is to be
found in this country, he has recently returned
from a visit to Brazil, Cuba, and Porto Rico, where
he went on the business of the Colonial Bank, and
where he availed himself of opportunities of collecting information relative to the Slave Trade.

He rates the Slave Trade of Brazil at   90,000
    Cuba and Porto Rico   .   .   100,000
    Captured in the year 1837   .   6,146
                                      ———
                                      196,146

Besides Texas, Buenos Ayres, and the Argentine
Republic, into which he believes there are large importations, though to what extent he has no means
of judging.

I now resort to a mode of proof totally different
from all the foregoing. I have had much commu-

nication with African merchants, engaged in legitimate trade; and it was suggested by one of them that a very fair estimate of numbers might be formed, from the amount of goods, prepared for the Slave Trade, (and absolutely inapplicable to any other purpose except the Slave Trade,) manufactured in this country. At my request, they furnished me with the following very intelligent summary of the argument, prepared, as I understood, by Captain M'Lean:—

It is necessarily impossible, from the very nature of the Slave Trade, to ascertain directly, or with any degree of precision, the number of slaves actually exported from the coast of Africa for the Transatlantic slave-markets, in any given year or space of time. But it is very possible, by instituting careful and minute inquiries into the several ramifications into which that traffic branches, to obtain results, by the combination of which we may arrive at an approximation to the truth, sufficiently accurate for all the purposes of the main inquiry. And if we find that the *data*, thus obtained from the most opposite sources, and from parties upon whose judgment and veracity the most implicit reliance may be placed, bring us to the same general result, it may, we think, be fairly taken for granted that that result is substantially correct.

Among the various sources to which we have applied ourselves, in order to ascertain the present actual extent of the Slave Trade, not the least important or satisfactory in its results has been a careful inquiry as to the quantity and value of goods manufactured expressly and exclusively for the purchase of slaves. The grounds upon which we instituted and carried on this investigation were these:—

1. We ascertained, by the concurrent testimony of competent and unimpeachable authority, that the merchandise chiefly, if not exclusively, given in exchange for slaves, consisted of cowries, Brazilian tobacco in rolls, spirits, and Manchester piece-goods.

D

2. That the *proportions* of the goods thus paid might be taken generally to be,—one-third cowries, a third tobacco and spirits, and a third Manchester cotton goods.

3. We ascertained that the *average* sum paid for each slave (taking the goods at cost prices) was about £4 sterling.

Lastly, we ascertained that all, or nearly all, the cotton goods purchased for the Slave Trade, were manufactured in Lancashire; and that the description of goods so manufactured were altogether unsuitable for any other market save that traffic alone.

Assuming these premises to be correct, and we verified them with much care, and by the most strict investigation, it of course followed that, if, by any means, we could ascertain, even proximately, the value and quantity of the cotton goods manufactured in, and exported from, Lancashire, for the Slave Trade, during any one of the last few years, we should arrive at a proximate (but, in the main, correct) estimate of the number of slaves actually purchased on the coast of Africa.

To some, this indirect *modus probandi*, as to an important fact, may appear far-fetched; but we are assured by those who are most conversant with the African trade generally, as well as with the Slave Trade and its operations in particular, that it is much more conclusive than, to those unacquainted with that peculiar trade, it would appear. As corroborative of other proofs, at least, it must certainly be regarded as very valuable.

From returns with which we have been furnished by parties whose names, were we at liberty to mention them, would be a sufficient guarantee for their correctness, we have ascertained that the entire quantity of cotton goods manufactured in Lancashire, for the African trade (including the legitimate, as well as the Slave Trade), was, in the year 1836, as follows :—

Value of Manchester goods manufactured exclusively for the African legitimate trade . £150,000

Value of goods manufactured in Lancashire, and shipped to Brazil, Cuba, United States, and elsewhere, intended for the Slave Trade, and adapted *only* for that trade . . . £250,000

Thus showing an excess in the quantity of goods manufactured for the Slave Trade, over that intended for legitimate trade, during the year 1836, of £100,000, or two-fifths of the whole amount.

Calculating by the *data* already given, we shall find that the number of slaves to the purchase of which the above amount of goods (manufactured and exported in one year, 1836) was adequate, would amount to the large number of 187,500,—a number which we have strong reason to believe, according to information derived from other sources, to be substantially correct.

Assuming the data on which the merchants calculate to be correct, some considerable addition must be made to the number of 187,500.

1. Goods only suited for the Slave Trade are manufactured at Glasgow as well as in Lancashire.

2. Specie to a very considerable extent finds its way through Cuba and Brazil to Africa, and is there employed in the purchase of Slaves. To the number then purchased by goods must be added the number purchased by money.

3. Ammunition and fire-arms to a large amount, and, like the goods, of a quality only fit for the Slave Trade, are sent from this country to Africa. The annual amount of such exports is stated in the Official Tables,* No. 6, of 1836, to be 137,698*l.* This item alone would give an increase of 34,174.

4. The Americans also furnish Cuba and Brazil with arms, ammunition, and goods.

5. East Indian goods also are employed in the Slave Trade.

It is superfluous to quote authority for the facts just enumerated, as they are notorious to commercial

---

* Tables of revenue, &c., published by authority of Parliament.

men. Thus, by the aid of this circumstantial evidence, of scarcely inferior value to direct and immediate proof, we show that the Slave Trade between Africa and the West cannot be less than 200,000, and probably reaches 250,000, annually imported.

There is also another mode of looking at the same question, though under an aspect quite distinct.

From an examination of the number of slaveships which left Brazil, Cuba, &c., in the year 1829,* as compared with the number captured in the same year, it appears that on the average, one in thirty, only, is taken; now, on the average of the years 1836 and 1837, we have 7538 négroes as the number captured, which being multiplied by 30, gives a total, 226,140.

Thus, then, the estimate of 150,000 at which, on the authority, principally, of the British Commissioners, I have myself arrived, with the number which perish on the passage,† make together an amount, which corresponds with, and is confirmed, 1st, by the actual observation of the

Governor of Cape Coast Castle, coupled with other authorities, by which the number must amount to   . .   200,000

2ndly, by Mr. M'Queen's researches, by which the number must amount to   196,000

3rdly, by the estimates founded on the quantity of goods exported for the

* Mr. M'Queen communicated this to me, last year.

† See Summary—Mortality, Middle Passage, p. 144.

Slave Trade, by which it must amount
to, from . . . 200,000 to 250,000
4thly, by a comparison between the proportion captured with those who escape, by which it must amount to . 226,000

I have now to consider the

MOHAMMEDAN SLAVE TRADE.

Hitherto, I have confined my observations to the
traffic across the Atlantic, from the east and west
coasts of Africa; there is yet another drain upon this
unhappy country, in the immense trade which is carried on for the supply of the Mohammedan markets
of Morocco, Tunis, Tripoli, Egypt, Turkey, Persia,
Arabia, and the borders of Asia.

This commerce comprises two distinct divisions,
1st, the maritime, the victims of which are shipped
from the north-east coast, in Arab vessels, and
2nd, the Desert, which is carried on, by means of
caravans, to Barbary, Egypt, &c.

The maritime trade is principally conducted by
the subjects of the Imaum of Muskat; and as this is
a branch of our subject, heretofore but little known,
I will make a few remarks as to its extent, the
countries which it supplies, and the amount of its
annual export.

Captain Cogan, of the Indian Navy, who, from
his frequent intercourse with the Imaum, and from
having been his accredited agent in England, had
the best opportunities of becoming acquainted with

this Prince and his subjects, has informed me that the Imaum's African dominions extend from Cape Delgado, about 1C° S. Lat., to the Rio dos Fuegos, under the Line; and that formerly this coast was notorious, for its traffic in slaves, with Christians as well as Mohammedans; the River Lindy, and the Island of Zanzebar, being the principal marts for the supply of the Christian market.

In 1822, a treaty was concluded by Captain Moresby, R.N., on behalf of the British Government, with the Imaum, by which the trade with Christian countries was declared abolished for ever, throughout his dominions and dependencies; but this arrangement, it must be remembered, does not in any way touch upon the Slave Trade carried on by the Imaum's subjects, with those of their own faith.

By means of this reserved trade, slaves are exported to Zanzebar; to the ports on both sides of the Arabian Gulf; to the markets of Egypt, Cairo, and Alexandria; to the south part of Arabia; to both sides of the Persian Gulf; to the north-west coasts of India; to the island of Java, and to most of the Eastern islands. The vessels which convey these negroes are in general the property of Arabs, or other Mohammedan traders.

Both Sir Alexander Johnston, who was long resident at Ceylon in a judicial situation, and Captain Cogan, have heard the number, thus exported, reckoned at 50,000 per annum; but Captain Cogan admits 20,000 to be the number legally exported from Africa, upon which the Imaum derives a revenue of so much per head; and he also admits that there is, besides, an illicit trade, by which 10,000 more may be smuggled every year.

All travellers who have recently visited the chief seats of this traffic, agree in describing it as very considerable.

" At Muskat," says Lieutenant Wellsted,* "about 4000 slaves of both sexes, and all ages, are disposed of annually."

Captain Cook, (to whom I have already referred,) who returned, in 1838, from a trading voyage to the eastern coast of Africa, informs me, that he was at Zanzebar at several different periods, and that he always "found the slave-market, held there daily, fully supplied. He could not ascertain the number annually sold, but slaves were constantly arriving in droves, of from 50 to 100 each, and found a ready sale ; they were chiefly," he understood, "purchased by Arab merchants, for the supply of Egypt, Abyssinia, Arabia, and the ports along the Arabian Gulf, to the markets of which countries hundreds were carried off and sold daily."

Many, however, are kept in Zanzebar, where there are sugar and spice plantations, and where, according to Ruschenberger,† the population amounts to 150,000, of which about two-thirds are slaves.

I also find, from Lieutenant Wellsted‡, that there

* Wellsted's Travels in Arabia &c., vol. i. p. 388.
† Ruschenberger's Voyage, 1835, 6, 7. vol. i. p. 40.
‡ Wellsted's Travels in Arabia, &c., vol. ii. p. 363.

is a Slave Trade carried on with the opposite coast of Arabia by the Somaulys, who inhabit the coast of Berbera, between Cape Guardafui and the Straits of Babel Mandel.

I am therefore warranted in taking Captain Cogan's estimate, viz., 30,000 per annum, as the number of negroes annually drained off by the Mohammedan Slave Trade from the east coast of Africa.*

I now come to the other division, that of the Desert, or caravan Slave Trade ; and here I shall briefly notice the countries which furnish its victims, so that we may see how vast a region lies under its withering influence.

By the laws of the Koran, no Mohammedan is allowed to enslave one of his own faith. The powerful Negro Moslem kingdoms, south of the desert, are thus, in a great measure, freed from the evils of this commerce; and the countries from which it is supplied are almost entirely Pagan, or only partially

---

* There seems also to be an export of slaves from the Portuguese settlements on the east coast of Africa to their possessions in Hindustan, which, as appears from the accounts of travellers, commenced towards the close of the seventeenth century, and has continued to the present time. In a dispatch to the Court of Directors from the Bombay Government, dated 12th May, 1838, Mr. Erskine, resident at Kattywar (in the province of Guzerat), states, that " a considerable importation of slaves takes place, at Dieu, both directly from the Arabian Gulf, and from Goa, and Dumaun, from whence they are brought into the province. For this I may confidently say, I see no remedy whatever, as it rests entirely with the British Government to say how far they consider it politic to interfere with their allies the Portuguese on this important question."

Mohammedan, and comprehend, in addition to the Pagan tribes (chiefly Tibboos), which are scattered over parts of the Desert, and lie intermixed among the Moslem kingdoms, all the northern part of Pagan Negroland, reaching, in a continuous line, from the banks of the Senegal to the mountains of Abyssinia and the sources of the Nile. The Negro Mohammedans, though not themselves sufferers from this Slave Trade, are active agents in carrying it on.

The Mohammedan towns of Jenné, Timbuctoo ; Kano and Sackatoo, in Houssa ; Kouka and Angornou, in Bornou ; Wawa, or Ware, the capital of Waday; and Cobbe the capital of Darfour,—are so many large warehouses, where the stores of human merchandise are kept for the supply of the Arab carriers or traders, who convey them in caravans across the Desert. The Soudan* negroes, so conveyed, and by many different routes,† are not only intended for the supply of Barbary and Egypt, and the banks of the Nile, from its mouth to the southern frontiers of Abyssinia, but, as I have learnt from a variety of authorities, they are exported to Turkey, Arabia, Syria, Persia, and Bokhara.‡

* The term " Soudan" is chiefly applied to the countries lying to the south of the Saharra or Great Desert.

† The great posts on the northern side of the Desert, where the traders collect, appear to be Wednoon, Tafilet, Fez, and Ghadanies ; Mourzouk, the capital of Fezzan ; and Siout and Shendy, on the Nile.

‡ The Hon. Mountstuart Elphinstone, in his account of Caubul (London, 1839, vol. i. p. 318), says, "there are slaves in Afghanistan : Abyssinians and Negroes are sometimes brought from Arabia."

With regard to the number thus annually exported, the absence of official documents, the imperfect evidence afforded by the statements of African travellers, and the immense extent of the subject itself, in its geographical relations, render it extremely difficult to obtain anything approaching to a correct estimate.

For these reasons, and as I have no wish to go beyond the bounds of producible proofs, I shall not estimate the Mohammedan Slave Trade at a greater extent than that which I am fairly entitled to assume, from the observations of African travellers.

Jackson, in his Travels in Africa,* speaks of a caravan from Timbuctoo to Tafilet, in 1805, consisting of "2000 persons, and 1800 camels."

Riley tells us,† that the Moor, Sidi Hamet, informed him, that in one yearly caravan with which he travelled (1807), from Timbuctoo to Morocco, there were 2000 slaves.

Captain Lyon ‡ gives 5000 or 5500, as the annual import into Fezzan; and Ritchie §, who travelled with him, says, that in 1819, 5000 slaves arrived at Mourzouk from Soudan.

Ritter ‖, in his observations on the Slave Trade, tells us, that the Darfour caravans arrive yearly at Cairo, from the interior, varying in their numbers ac-

* Jackson's Travels, 1809, p. 239. † Riley's Narrative, p. 382.
‡ Lyon's Narrative. London, 1821, pp. 188, 189.
§ Ritchie, quoted in the Quarterly Review, 1820, No. 45, p. 228.
‖ A German, who published a geographical work in 1820, p. 380.

cording to time and circumstances; the smaller caravans, consisting of from 5000 to 6000 (according to Browne,* only 1000); the larger, which however do not often arrive, of about 12,000.† Far fewer come down the Nile with the Senaar caravan, and only a few, from Bornou through Fezzan, by the Maugraby caravan, although hunting-parties are fitted out in Bornou, against the negroes, in the adjoining highlands.

Browne, who resided in Darfour three years, about the end of the last century, says, that in the caravan with which he travelled through the Desert to Cairo, there were 5000 slaves.‡

Burkhardt, who travelled in Nubia, &c., in 1814, informs us,§ that 5000 slaves are annually sold in the market of Shendy, " of whom 2500 are carried off by the Souakin merchants, and 1500 by those of Egypt; the remainder go to Dongola and the Bedouins, who live to the east of Shendy, towards Akbara and the Red Sea;" and he afterwards says,‖ " Souakin, upon the whole, may be considered as one of the first Slave Trade markets in eastern Africa; it imports annually, from Shendy and Senaar, from 2000 to 3000 slaves, equalling nearly, in this respect, Esne and Siout, in Egypt, and Massouah in Abys-

* Browne's Travels, 1793, p. 246.

† Mémoires sur L'Egypte, tom. iii., p. 303. Lapanouse, iv. p. 77.

‡ Pinkerton's Voyages, &c. Vol. xv. p. 155.

§ Burkhardt's Travels, p. 324. ‖ Ib. p. 442.

sinia, where, as I afterwards learnt at Djidda, there is an annual transit from the interior of about 3500 slaves. From these four points, from the southern harbours of Abyssinia, and from the Somauly and Mozambique coast, it may be computed, that Egypt and Arabia draw an annual supply of 15,000 or 20,000 slaves, brought from the interior of Africa."*

Colonel Leake, who was in Egypt a few years ago, has informed me, that besides the supply from Shendy, noticed by Burkhardt, Cairo derives an additional number of 5000 annually, which are brought to the market there, from Soudan, by other routes.

Dr. Holroyd, who has lately returned from travelling in Nubia and Kordofan, has stated that the Pacha of Egypt's troops bring into Kordofan captives from his northern frontiers, to the amount of 7000 or 8000 annually; that about one-half so introduced are retained for the use of the army and the inhabitants, while the other half are sold to the merchants of Shendy and Siout: that 5000 negroes,

---

* In the ' Times' newspaper of the 14th February, 1839, I find that on the evening of the 11th, at the meeting of the Royal Geographical Society, " the paper read was, an account of the survey of the south-east coast of Arabia by Captain Haines of the Indian navy." After describing Aden, he says, " the next town of importance is Mokhara, containing about 4500 inhabitants, with a very considerable trade, particularly in slaves. The writer has seen exposed for sale in the market, at one time, no less than 700 Nubian girls, subject to all the brutality and insults of their masters; the prices which they fetch varying from 7l. to 25l.

annually, reach Cairo by Es Souan, but that others also are brought there from Abyssinia by the Red Sea, and from Darfour, by the Desert; and that slaves are conveyed from Senaar, by three separate routes, in daily caravans, varying in extent from 5 to 200. Dr. Holroyd visited the governor of Kordofan in 1837; he had then just returned from a " gasoua," (slave-hunt) at Gibel Nooba, the product of which was 2187 negroes. From these, " the physician to the forces was selecting able-bodied men for the army; but so repeatedly has the Pacha waged war against this chain of mountains, that the population has been completely drained, and from the above number, only 250 men were deemed fit for military service." *

Dr. Bowring, who visited Egypt in 1837, has informed me, that he estimates the annual importation of slaves into Egypt at from 10,000 to 12,000; that the arrivals in Kordofan amount to about the same number: that in 1827, a single caravan brought 2820 slaves to Siout, but that, in general, the annual arrivals there fluctuate between 500 and 5000; and that such is the facility of introducing slaves, that they "now filtrate into Egypt by almost daily arrivals."

From the authorities which I have now given, I think I may fairly estimate the northern or Desert portion of the Mohammedan Slave Trade at 20,000 per annum.

I am aware that this amount is far below the

* Statement by Dr. Holroyd, yet unpublished.

numbers given by others who are well acquainted with the subject; for example, the eminent eastern traveller, Count de Laborde, estimates the number that are annually carried into slavery from East Soudan, Abyssinia, &c. at 30,000. He also tells us that, in the kingdom of Darfour, an independent Slave Trade is carried on;* and Burkhardt states, that Egypt and Arabia together, draw an annual supply of from 15,000 to 20,000 from the same countries; but having no desire to depart from the rule I have laid down, of stating nothing upon conjecture, however reasonable that conjecture may be, I shall not take more than

For the Desert trade . . . . . 20,000†
which, added to the annual export from the
eastern coast, proved to be . . . 30,000
_____

gives the number of 50,000
as the annual amount of the Mohammedan Slave Trade.‡

---

* Chasse aux Nègres. Leon de Laborde. Paris, Dupont et Cie., 1838, pp. 14 and 17.

† The following are some of these authorities :—

1st. For the number exported annually from Soudan
  to Morocco, &c., I take Jackson and Riley at . . 2000
2nd. From Soudan to Mourzouk, Lyon and Ritchie give 5000
3rd. From Abyssinia to Arabia, &c., Burkhardt, says about 3500
4th. From Abyssinia, Kordofan, and Darfour, to Egypt,
  Arabia, &c., I take Browne, Burkhardt, Col. Leake,
  Count de Laborde, Dr. Holroyd, and Dr. Bowring, at 12,000
  _____

  Total for Desert trade 22,500

‡ It ought to be borne in mind, that I have not taken into the account the number of slaves which are required for the home

SUMMARY.

Such, then, is the arithmetic of the case ; and I earnestly solicit my reader, before he proceeds further, to come to a verdict in his own mind, upon slavery of the Mohammedan provinces and kingdoms in Central Africa. These are very extensive and populous, and travellers inform us that the bulk of their population is composed of slaves. We have therefore the powerful nations of Houssa (including the Felatahs), Bornou, Begarmi, and Darfour, all draining off from Soudan annual supplies of negroes, for domestic and agricultural purposes, besides those procured for the foreign trade. On this head, Burkhardt says[1] " I have reason to believe, however, that the numbers exported from Soudan to Egypt and Arabia bears only a small proportion to those kept by the Mussulmen of the southern countries themselves, or, in other words, to the whole number yearly derived by purchase or by force from the nations in the interior of Africa. At Berber and Shendy there is scarcely a house which does not possess one or two slaves, and five or six are frequently seen in the same family ; the great people and chiefs keep them by dozens. As high up the Nile as Senaar, the same system prevails, as well as westwards to Kordofan, Darfour, and thence towards Bornou. All the Bedouin tribes, also, who surround those countries are well stocked with slaves. If we may judge of their numbers by those kept on the borders of the Nile, (and I was assured by the traders that slaves were more numerous in those distant countries than even at Shendy,) it is evident that the number exported towards Egypt, Arabia, and Barbary, is very greatly below what remains within the limits of Soudan." He then states that, from his own observation, the slaves betwixt Berber and Shendy amount to not less than 12,000, and that, probably, there are 20,000 slaves in Darfour ; " and every account agrees in proving that as we proceed further westward, into the populous countries of Dar Saley, Bornou, Bagarmè, and the king-doms of Afnou and Houssa, the proportion of the slave population does not diminish."

[1] Burkhardt, p. 340.

the fairness and accuracy of these figures. I am aware that it requires far more than ordinary patience to wade through this mass of calculation; I have, however, resolved to present this part of the subject in its dry and uninviting form, partly from utter despair of being able, by any language I could use, to give an adequate image of the extent, variety, and intensity of human suffering, which must exist if these figures be true; and partly from the belief that a bare arithmetical detail, free from whatever could excite the imagination or distress the feelings, is best fitted to carry conviction along with it. I then ask, is the calculation a fair one? Some may think that there is exaggeration in the result, and others may complain that I have been too rigorous in striking off every equivocal item, and have made my estimate as if it were my object and desire, as far as possible, to reduce the sum total. It signifies little to the argument, whether the error be on the one side or the other; but it is of material importance that the reader, for the purpose of following the argument, should now fix and ascertain the number which seems to him the reasonable and moderate result from the facts and figures which have been produced. To me, it seems just to take, annually,

For the Christian Slave Trade	. .	150,000
For the Mohammedan	. . . .	50,000
Making a total of	. .	200,000

MORTALITY.

HITHERTO, I have stated less than the half of this dreadful case. I am now going to show that, besides the 200,000 annually carried into captivity, there are claims on our compassion for almost countless cruelties and murders growing out of the Slave Trade. I am about to prove that this multitude of our enslaved fellow men is but the remnant of numbers vastly greater, the survivors of a still larger multitude, over whom the Slave Trade spreads its devastating hand, and that for every ten who reach Cuba or Brazil, and become available as slaves,—fourteen, at least, are destroyed.

This mortality arises from the following causes :—

1. The original seizure of the slaves.

2. The march to the coast, and detention there.

3. The middle passage.

4. The sufferings after capture, and after landing. And

5. The initiation into slavery, or the " seasoning," as it is termed by the planters.

It will be necessary for me to make a few remarks on each of these heads ; and 1st, As to the mortality incident to the period of

E

Seizure.

"The whole, or the greater part of that immense continent, is a field of warfare and desolation; a wilderness, in which the inhabitants are wolves to each other." — *Speech of Bryan Edwards.*

On the authority of public documents, parliamentary evidence, and the works of African travellers, it appears that the principal and almost the only cause of war in the interior of Africa, is the desire to procure slaves for traffic; and that every species of violence, from the invasion of an army, to that of robbery by a single individual, is had recourse to, for the attainment of this object.

Lord Muncaster, in his able historical sketches of the Slave Trade,* in which he gives us an analysis of the evidence taken before the Privy Council and the House of Commons about the year 1790, clearly demonstrates the truth of my assertion, at the period when he published his work (1792); and the authorities from that time, down to the present day, as clearly show, that the most revolting features of the Slave Trade, in this respect, (at least, as regards the native chiefs and slave-traders of Africa,) have continued to exist, and do now exist.

Bruce, who travelled in Abyssinia in 1770, in describing the slave-hunting expeditions there, says: "The grown-up men are all killed, and are then mutilated, parts of their bodies being always carried away as trophies; several of the old mothers are

* Lord Muncaster's Historical Sketches. London, 1792.

also killed, while others, frantic with fear and despair, kill themselves. The boys and girls of a more tender age are then carried off in brutal triumph." *

Mr. Wilberforce, in his letter to his constituents in 1807,† has described the mode in which slaves are usually obtained in Africa, and he quotes several passages from the work of the enterprising traveller, Mungo Park, bearing particularly on this subject. Park says, " The king of Bambarra having declared war against Kaarta, and dividing his army into small detachments, overran the country, and seized on the inhabitants before they had time to escape; and in a few days the whole kingdom of Kaarta became a scene of desolation. This attack was soon retaliated; Daisy, the king of Kaarta, took with him 800 of his best men, and surprised, in the night, three large villages near Kooniakary, in which many of his traitorous subjects had taken up their residence; all these, and indeed all the able men who fell into Daisy's hands, were immediately put to death."‡ Mr. Wilberforce afterwards says: " In another part of the country, we learn from the most respectable testimony, that a practice prevails, called ' village-breaking.' It is precisely the ' tegria' of Mr. Park, with this difference, that, though often

* Bruce's Travels in Abyssinia.
† Wilberforce's Letter on the Abolition of the Slave Trade. London. 1807, p. 392.
‡ Park's Travels, London, 1817, vol. i. p. 164.

termed making war, it is acknowledged to be practised for the express purpose of obtaining victims for
the slave-market. The village is attacked in the
night; if deemed needful, to increase the confusion,
it is set on fire, and the wretched inhabitants, as
they are flying naked from the flames, are seized
and carried into slavery." " These depredations
are far more commonly perpetrated by the natives
on each other, and on a larger or smaller scale,
according to the power and number of the assailants,
and the resort of ships to the coast; it prevails so
generally as throughout the whole extent of Africa
to render person and property utterly insecure."*
And in another place, " Every man who has acquired any considerable property, or who has a
large family, the sale of which will produce a considerable profit, excites in the chieftain near whom
he resides the same longings which are called forth
in the wild beast by the exhibition of his proper prey;
and he himself lives in a continual state of suspicion
and terror."†

The statements of Mr. Wilberforce have been
corroborated by Mr. Bryan Edwards, (from whom
I have already quoted,) himself a dealer in slaves,
and an able and persevering advocate for the continuance of the traffic. In a speech delivered in
the Jamaica Assembly, he says, " I am persuaded
that Mr. Wilberforce has been very rightly informed
as to the manner in which slaves are very generally

---

* Wilberforce's Letter, &c., p. 23.　　† Ibid. p. 28.

procured. The intelligence I have collected from my own negroes abundantly confirms his account; and I have not the smallest doubt that in Africa the effects of this trade are precisely such as he represents them to be."

But it may be said, admitting these statements to be true, they refer to a state of things in Africa which does not *now* exist. A considerable period of time has indeed elapsed since these statements were made; but it clearly appears, that the same system has obtained, throughout the interior of Africa, down to the present time; nor is it to be expected that any favourable change will take place during the continuance of the slave-traffic.

Professor Smith, who accompanied Captain Tuckey in the expedition to the Congo in 1816, says, " Every man I have conversed with acknowledges that, if white men did not come for slaves, the wars, which nine times out of ten result from the European Slave Trade, would be proportionally less frequent." *

Captain Lyon states that, when he was at Fezzan in 1819, Mukni, the reigning Sultan, was continually engaged in these slave-hunts, in one of which 1800 were captured, all of whom, excepting a very few, either perished on their march before they reached Fezzan, or were killed by their captor.†

Major Gray, who travelled in the vicinity of the River Gambia, and Dupuis, who was British Consul

---

* Tuckey's Expedition, &c., p. 187.
† Lyon's Travels, p. 129.

at Ashantee about the same period, 1820, both agree in attributing the wars, which they knew to be frequent in the countries where they travelled, to the desire of procuring slaves for traffic.* Dupuis narrates a speech of the king of Ashantee. " Then my fetische made me strong, like my ancestors, and I killed Dinkera, and took his gold, and brought more than 20,000 slaves to Coomassy. Some of these people being bad men, I washed my stool in their blood for the fetische. But, then, some were good people, and these I sold or gave to my captains; many, moreover, died, because this country does not grow too much corn, like Sarem, and what can I do? Unless I kill or sell them, they will grow strong and kill my people. Now, you must tell my master (the King of England) that these slaves can work for him, and if he wants 10,000 he can have them."†

Captain Moresby, a naval officer, who was stationed on the eastern coast in 1821, and who had peculiar opportunities of learning the mode in which slaves were obtained, informed me that "The Arab traders, from the coast of Zanzebar, go up the country, provided with trinkets and beads, strung in various forms; thus they arrive at a point where little intercourse has taken place, and where the inhabitants are in a state of barbarism; here they display their beads and trinkets to the natives, according to the number of slaves they want. A certain

* Gray's Travels in Western Africa. London, 1825, p. 97.
† Dupuis' Residence in Ashantee. London, 1824, p. 164.

village is doomed to be surprised; in a short time
the Arabs have their choice of its inhabitants—
the old and infirm are either left to perish, or be
slaughtered."

In 1822 our Minister at Paris thus addressed
Count de Villèle : "There seems to be scarcely a spot
on that coast (from Sierra Leone to Cape Mount)
which does not show traces of the Slave Trade,
with all its attendant horrors ; for the arrival of a
ship, in any of the rivers on the windward coast,
being the signal for war between the natives, the
hamlets of the weaker party are burnt, and the
miserable survivors carried off and sold to the slave-
traders."

We have obtained most valuable information as to
the interior of Africa from the laborious exertions of
Denham and Clapperton. They reached Soudan, or
Nigritia, by the land-route through Fezzan and
Bornou, in 1823, and the narrative of their journey
furnishes many melancholy proofs of the miseries to
which Africa is exposed through the demands for the
Slave Trade. Major Denham says : " On attacking a
place, it is the custom of the country instantly to fire
it ; and, as they (the villages) are all composed of
straw huts only, the whole is shortly devoured by the
flames. The unfortunate inhabitants fly quickly
from the devouring element, and fall immediately
into the hands of their no less merciless enemies,
who surround the place ; the men are quickly mas-
sacred, and the women and children lashed together

and made slaves." * Denham then tells us that the
Begharmi nation had been discomfited by the Sheik of
Bornou " in five different expeditions, when at least
20,000 poor creatures were slaughtered, and three-
fourths of that number, at least, driven into slavery."†
And, in speaking of these wars, he uses this remarkable expression—" The season of the year had
arrived (25th November) when the sovereigns of
these countries go out to battle." He also narrates
the terms of an alliance betwixt the Sheik of
Bornou and the Sultan of Mandara. " This treaty
of alliance was confirmed by the Sheik's receiving in marriage the daughter of the Sultan, and
the marriage-portion was to be the produce of an
immediate expedition into the Kerdy country, by the
united forces of these allies. The results were as
favourable as the most savage confederacy could have
anticipated. Three thousand unfortunate wretches
were dragged from their native wilds, and sold to
perpetual slavery, while probably *double that number were sacrificed to obtain them.*"‡

Denham, himself, accompanied an expedition
against Mandara, one of the results of which was,
that the town, " Darkalla, was quickly burnt, and
another smaller town near it, and the few inhabitants who were found in them, chiefly infants and
aged persons, were put to death without mercy, and
thrown into the flames."§

* Denham and Clapperton's Travels, &c. in Africa. London,
1826, p. 164.   † Ib. p. 214.   ‡ Ib. p. 116.   § Ib. p. 131.

Commodore Owen, who was employed in the survey of the eastern coast of Africa about the years 1823 and 1824, says: "The riches of Quilimane consisted, in a trifling degree, of gold and silver, but principally of grain, which was produced in such quantities as to supply Mozambique. But the introduction of the Slave Trade stopped the pursuits of industry, and changed those places, where peace and agriculture had formerly reigned, into the seat of war and bloodshed. Contending tribes are now constantly striving to obtain, by mutual conflict, prisoners as slaves for sale to the Portuguese, who excite these wars, and fatten on the blood and wretchedness they produce."

In speaking of Inhambane, he says : "The slaves they do obtain are the spoils of war among the petty tribes, who, were it not for the market they thus find for their prisoners, would in all likelihood remain in peace with each other, and probably be connected by bonds of mutual interest." *

Mr. Ashmun, agent of the American Colonial Society, in writing to the Board of Directors, from Liberia, in 1823, says, "The following incident I relate, not for its singularity, for similar events take place, perhaps, every month in the year, but it has fallen under my own observation, and I can vouch for its authenticity :—King Boatswain, our most powerful supporter, and steady friend among the natives, (so he has uniformly shown

* Owen's Voyage, &c., vol. i. p. 287.

himself,) received a quantity of goods on trust from a French slaver, for which he stipulated to pay young slaves—he makes it a point of honour to be punctual to his engagements. The time was at hand when he expected the return of the slaver, and he had not the slaves. Looking around on the peaceable tribes about him for his victims, he singled out the Queaks, a small agricultural and trading people of most inoffensive character. His warriors were skilfully distributed to the different hamlets, and making a simultaneous assault on the sleeping occupants in the dead of the night, accomplished, without difficulty or resistance, in one hour, the annihilation of the whole tribe ;—every adult, man and woman, was murdered—every hut fired! Very young children, generally, shared the fate of their parents ; the boys and girls alone were reserved to pay the Frenchman." *

The Commissioners at Sierra Leone, in a despatch of April 10, 1825, speaking of a great increase in the Slave Trade, which had then lately taken place on the coast between that colony and the Gallinas, state that the increased demand for slaves conse- quent thereon was " the cause of the destructive war which had raged in the Sherbro' for the last eighteen months, between the ' Cassoos,' a powerful nation living in the interior, and the Fi people, and Sherbro' Bulloms, who live near the water-side, and are com- pletely under the influence of the slaving chiefs and

* Ashmun's Life. New York, 1835, p. 160.

factors settled in the neighbourhood." * The Cassoos
are represented as having carried fire, rapine, and
murder, throughout the different villages through
which they passed, most of the women and children
of which, together with the prisoners, were immediately sold to the slave-factors who were at hand to
receive them.

We have also, on this head, the more recent testimony of Lander and Laird. Lander accompanied
Clapperton from Badagry to Sockatoo, and on the
death of Clapperton he returned to Badagry, with
little variation, by the same route. In 1830 he was
sent out by the British Government to Africa, and
succeeded in navigating the Niger from Boossa,
where Park was drowned, to the sea, in the Bight of
Benin. In his journal, he observes that slavery has
" produced the most baleful effects, causing anarchy,
injustice, and oppression to reign in Africa, and
exciting nation to rise up against nation, and man
against man ; it has covered the face of the country
with desolation. All these evils, and many others,
has slavery accomplished; in return for which the
Europeans, for whose benefit, and by whose connivance and encouragement it has flourished so extensively, have given to the heartless natives ardent spirits, tawdry silk dresses, and paltry neck-
laces of beads."†

Laird ascended the Niger and its tributary the

* Class A, 1826, p. 7.
† Lander's Records. London, 1830, vol. i. p. 38.

Tschadda, in 1832, and was an eye-witness of the cruelties consequent on the Slave Trade, while in the river near to the confluence of the two streams. He says, speaking of the incursions of the Felatahs, " Scarcely a night passed, but we heard the screams of some unfortunate beings that were carried off into slavery by these villainous depredators. The inhabitants of the towns in the route of the Felatahs fled across the river on the approach of the enemy." " A few days after the arrival of the fugitives, a column of smoke rising in the air, about five miles above the confluence, marked the advance of the Felatahs; and in two days afterwards the whole of the towns, including Addah Cuddah, and five or six others, were in a blaze. The shrieks of the unfortunate wretches that had not escaped, answered by the loud wailings and lamentations of their friends and relations (encamped on the opposite bank of the river), at seeing them carried off into slavery, and their habitations destroyed, produced a scene, which, though *common enough in the country*, had seldom, if ever before, been witnessed by European eyes, and showed to me, in a more striking light than I had hitherto beheld it, the horrors attendant upon slavery." *

Rankin, in the narrative of his visit to Sierra Leone in 1833, says : The warlike Sherbros had recently invaded the territories of the Timmanees,

* Laird and Oldfield's Narrative. London, 1837, vol. i. pp. 149, 247.

and had fallen on the unguarded Rokel, which became a prey to the flames. "The inhabitants who could not escape across the river to Magbelly perished, or were made slaves, and the town was reduced to ashes." *

Colonel Nicolls, late Governor at Fernando Po, has informed me, that when he visited the town of Old Calebar in 1834, he found the natives boasting of a predatory excursion, in which they had recently been engaged, in which they had surprised a village, killed those who resisted, and carried off the remainder as slaves. In alluding to this excursion, Colonel Nicolls heard an African boy, who had formed one of the party, declare that he had killed three himself!

The Rev. Mr. Fox, a Wesleyan missionary at the Gambia, in a letter dated 13th March, 1837, addressed to the Secretary of the Wesleyan Missionary Society, says,—" I visited Jamalli a few weeks ago, and also Laming, another small Mandingo town, on the way: at the latter place I counted twelve huts that had been destroyed by fire, and at the former about forty. Proceeding to the Foulah town, about half a mile eastward, I found it was not in the least injured, but, like the other two, was without inhabitants; not a soul was to be seen."

" Foolokolong, a large Foulah town in Kimmington's dominions, has lately been attacked by Wooli, and, I believe, nearly the whole of it destroyed, the cattle driven away, many of the inhabitants

* Rankin's Sierra Leone. London, 1836, vol. ii. p. 259.

killed, and many others taken prisoners. On Wednesday evening last I returned from a hasty visit to the upper river. I went as far as Fattatenda. At Bannatenda, not quite half the way, I found a poor aged Foulah woman in irons, who, upon inquiry, I found was from Foolokolong, one of the many who were captured in the recent war, and that she was sent on the south side of the river to be sold, for a horse; I immediately rescued the half-famished and three-parts-naked female from the horrors of slavery by giving a good horse, broke off her chains, and brought her to this settlement, where, by a singular but happy coincidence, she met with her own brother (who lives upon Hattaba's land), who, hearing that she, her daughter, and daughter's children, had been taken in the war, had been a considerable way up the river to inquire after them, but heard nothing of them, and had consequently returned. I of course, gave the woman up to her brother, from whom, as well as herself, and several Foulahs who came to see her, I received a number of blessings."

In another part of the same letter he writes,— " From the king himself I learned that they brought 350 Foulahs from Foolokolong (Kimmington's largest Foulah town), besides 100 whom they killed on the spot."

In another letter, dated 5th January 1838, Mr. Fox says, " The Bambarras have proceeded a considerable distance down the north bank of the river (Gambia), have pillaged and destroyed several small towns, taken some of the inhabitants into slavery, and a few people have been killed."

" The neighbourhood of M'Carthy's Island is again in a very disturbed state. Scarcely are the rains over, and the produce of a plentiful harvest gathered in, ere the noise of battle and the din of warfare is heard at a distance, with all its attendant horrors ; mothers, snatching up their children with a few necessary articles, flee for their lives ; towns, after being pillaged of as much cattle, &c., as the banditti require, are immediately set on fire ; columns of smoke ascend the heavens ; the cries of those who are being butchered may be more easily conceived than expressed ; and those who escape destruction are carried into the miseries of hopeless slavery. A number of Bambarras are again on the north bank of the river, not far from this place, and the poor Foulahs at Jamalli have consequently fled to this island for protection, bringing with them as many of their cattle, and other things, as they could."

The Rev. Mr. M'Brair, another Wesleyan missionary, who has seen much of the interior of Africa, in the vicinity of the Gambia, from which he has recently returned to this country, makes the following observations, in a letter also to the Secretary of the Wesleyan Missionary Society :

" On other occasions a party of men-hunters associate together, and, falling suddenly upon a small town or village during the night, they massacre all the men that offer any resistance, and carry away the rest of the inhabitants as the best parts of their spoil. Or, when a chieftain thinks himself sufficiently powerful, he makes the most frivolous excuses for waging war upon his neighbour, so that he may spoil his country of its inhabitants. Having been in close connexion with many of the liberated Africans in M'Carthy's Island, 250 miles up the Gambia, and also in St. Mary's, at the mouth of that river, we had many opportunities of learning the various modes in which they had been captured; from which it appeared that the wholesale method of seizure is by far the most frequent, and that, without this plan, a sufficient number of victims could not be procured for the market; so that it may be called the prevailing way of obtaining slaves."

" Whilst I was in M'Carthy's Island, a capture took place at the distance of half a day's journey from my abode. The king of Woolli, on a very slight pretence, fell upon a village during the night, slew six men, and carried off forty captives. The inhabitants also of a neighbouring place were destined to the same fate, but having had timely notice of his approach, they saved themselves by a precipitous flight, and M'Carthy's Island was filled for a time with refugees from all the country round about."

The Rev. Mr. Morgan, another Wesleyan missionary, lately from the Gambia, writes to the Secretary as follows :—" I feel confident that the Slave Trade has established feuds among them (the African tribes around the Gambia), by which they will be embroiled in war for generations to come, unless the disposition be destroyed by the Christian religion, or their circumstances be changed by civilization."

I must not leave this part of my subject without calling attention to the extraordinary facts which have recently been made public, regarding the practices of the Pacha of Egypt, and the chiefs in Nubia and Darfour. There has been revealed to us a new feature in the mode of procuring negroes for slaves; and we find that troops regularly disciplined are, at stated seasons, led forth to hunt down and harry the defenceless inhabitants of Eastern Nigritia.

In a despatch from Lieutenant-Colonel Campbell, Her Majesty's Consul at Cairo, of date 1st December 1837,* we are informed that the Consul waited on Mahommed Ali, and communicated to him " that statements had gone home to the Government and people of England, from eye-witnesses, that slave-hunts (*gazoua*) had been carried on by the officers and the troops of the pacha; that large numbers of negroes had been taken, and had been distributed among the soldiers, in liquidation of the arrears of their pay; that on one occasion the gazoua had collected 2700 slaves, of whom 250 had been forced among the ranks of his army, and the remainder had been divided among the officers and soldiers at fixed prices, according to the state of their arrears."

The pacha professed not to know that his army had been employed in slave-hunts for the purpose

* Class B, Farther Series, 1837, p. 69.

F

of discharging arrears of pay; but he admitted he was aware that his officers had carried on the Slave Trade for their own account, " a conduct of which he by no means approved." We have no farther particulars in this important despatch: but the enterprise of a traveller, Count De Laborde, who has lately returned from Nubia and Egypt, will enable me to introduce those of my readers who have not seen his work,* to the scenes of cruelty and devastation perpetrated by the pacha's troops, which he has graphically described.

The narrative, of which I can only give a brief outline, was communicated to him by a French officer, who went to Cairo in 1828, and resided ten years in Egypt.

M. —— there learnt that four expeditions, called gaswahs, annually set out from Obeid, the capital of Kordofan, towards the south, to the mountains inhabited by the Nubas negroes. The manner and object of their departure are thus described: " One day he heard a great noise; the whole village appeared in confusion; the cavalry were mounted, and the infantry discharging their guns in the air, and increasing the uproar with their still more noisy hurras. M. ——, on inquiring the cause of the rejoicing, was exultingly told by a follower of the troop, " It is the gaswah." " The gaswah! for what—gazelles?" " Yes, gazelles; here are the nets, ropes, and chains; they are to be brought home

* Chasse aux Nègres, Leon De Laborde, Paris, 1838.

alive." On the return of the expedition, all the
people went out, singing and dancing, to meet the
hunters. M. ——— went out also, wishing to join in
the rejoicing. He told Count Laborde he never could
forget the scene presented to his eyes. What did he
see ? What gain did these intrepid hunters, after
twenty days of toil, drag after them ? Men in chains ;
old men carried on litters, because unable to walk ;
the wounded dragging their weakened limbs with
pain, and a multitude of children following their
mothers, who carried the younger ones in their
arms. Fifteen hundred negroes, corded, naked, and
wretched, escorted by 400 soldiers in full array. This
was the gaswah. These the poor gazelles taken
in the Desert. He himself afterwards accompanied
one of these gaswahs. The expedition consisted of
400 Egyptian soldiers, 100 Bedouin cavalry, and
twelve village chiefs, with peasants carrying provisions. On arriving at their destination, which
they generally contrive to do before dawn, the cavalry
wheel round the mountain, and by a skilful movement form themselves into a semi-circle on one side,
whilst the infantry enclose it on the other. The negroes, whose sleep is so profound that they seldom
have time to provide for their safety, are thus completely entrapped. At sunrise the troops commence
operations by opening a fire on the mountain with
musketry and cannon ; immediately the heads of the
wretched mountaineers may be seen in all directions,
among the rocks and trees, as they gradually retreat,

dragging after them the young and infirm. Four detachments armed with bayonets, are then despatched up the mountain in pursuit of the fugitives, whilst a continual fire is kept up from the musketry and cannon below, which are loaded only with powder, as their object is rather to dismay than to murder the inhabitants. The more courageous natives, however, make a stand by the mouths of the caves, dug for security against their enemies. They throw their long poisoned javelins, covering themselves with their shields, while their wives and children stand by them and encourage them with their voices; but when the head of the family is killed, they surrender without a murmur. When struck by a ball, the negro, ignorant of the nature of the wound, may generally be seen rubbing it with earth till he falls through loss of blood. The less courageous fly with their families to the caves, whence the hunters expel them by firing pepper into the hole. The negroes, almost blinded and suffocated, run into the snares previously prepared, and are put in irons. If after the firing no one makes his appearance, the hunters conclude that the mothers have killed their children, and the husbands their wives and themselves. When the negroes are taken, their strong attachment to their families and lands is apparent. They refuse to stir, some clinging to the trees with all their strength, while others embrace their wives and children so closely, that it is necessary to separate them with the sword; or they are bound to a horse, and are dragged over brambles and rocks until they reach the foot of the mountain, bruised, bloody, and disfigured. If they still continue obstinate, they are put to death.

Each detachment, having captured its share of the spoil, returns to the main body, and is succeeded by others, until the mountain, " de battue en battue," is depopulated. If from the strength of the position, or the obstinacy of the resistance, the first assault is unsuccessful, the General adopts the inhuman expedient of reducing them by thirst; this is easily effected by encamping above the springs at the foot of the mountain, and thus cutting off their only supply of water. The miserable negroes often endure this siege for a week; and may be seen gnawing the bark of trees to extract a little moisture, till at length they are compelled to exchange their country, liberty, and families, for a drop of water. They every day approach nearer, and retreat on seeing the soldiers, until the temptation of the water shown them becomes too strong to be resisted. At length they submit to have the manacles fastened on their hands, and a heavy fork suspended to their necks, which they are obliged to lift at every step.

The march from the Nuba mountains to Obeid is short. From thence they are sent to Cairo. There the pacha distributes them as he thinks proper; the aged, infirm, and wounded, are given to the Bedouins, who are the most merciless of masters, and exact their due of hard labour with a severity proportioned to the probable short duration of the lives of their unhappy victims.

At Obeid alone 6000 human beings are annually dragged into slavery, and that at the cost of 2000 more, who are killed in the capture. The king of Darfur also imports for sale yearly 8000 or 9000 slaves, a fourth of whom usually die during the fatigues of a forced march: they are compelled, by the scarcity of provisions, to hurry forward with all speed. In vain the exhausted wretches supplicate for one day's rest; they have no alternative but to push on, or be left behind a prey to the hungry jackals and hyænas. " On one occasion," says the narrator, " when, a few days after the march of a caravan, I rapidly crossed the same desert, mounted on a fleet dromedary, I found my way by the newly-mangled human carcasses, and by them I was guided to the nightly halt."

Dr. Holroyd, whom I have already mentioned, in a letter to me, of date 14th January 1839, says, in reference to these " gazouas," of the Egyptian troops, " I should think, if my information be correct, that, in addition to 7000 or 8000 taken captive, at least 1500 were killed in defence or by suffocation at the time of being taken ; for I learnt that, when the blacks saw the troops advancing, they took refuge in caves ; the soldiers then fired into the caverns, and, if this did not induce them to quit their places of concealment, they made fires at the entrances, and either stifled the negroes, or compelled them to surrender. Where this latter method of taking them was adopted, it was not an uncommon circumstance to see a female with a child at her breast, who had been wounded by a musket-ball, staggering from her hiding-place, and dying immediately after her exit."*

* In the same letter, dated January 14, 1839, Dr. Holroyd having mentioned that he had " brought from Kordofan, at his own request, a negro (an intelligent boy) about twelve years of age, who had been seized by Mahomed Ali's troops from Gebel Noobah, and from whom all particulars can be obtained in reference to that inhuman method of taking the blacks," I asked that the boy might be questioned as to what he had seen of the slave-hunts. Dr. Holroyd has favoured me with the following " Statement of Almas, a negro boy taken in the gazzua of Gebel Noobah, three years ago, by the troops of Mahomed Ali Pacha. Almas is a native of Korgo, a very considerable district on the south side of Gebel Noobah; it is governed by a sheik, who is under the command of a local sultan. He was living at Korgo at the time of his capture, and says, that the pacha's troops made the attack during the night, whilst the negroes were sleeping; that they fired repeatedly upon the district with cannon and muskets, both loaded with shot; and that they burnt the straw huts of the negroes. As they escaped from their burning huts they were seized by the troops: many, especially the children, were burnt to death, and many were killed. Those who ran away, and were pursued by the soldiers, defended themselves with stones, spears, and trombashes; the latter, an iron weapon in common use among the natives of these mountains.

" The negroes retreated to the caves in the sides of the mountains, from whence they were eventually obliged to come forth, from fear of suffocation from the fires made at the entrances, or from want of food and water. He never heard of pepper, mentioned by Laborde, as having been used in loading the guns, or of firing it into the caves to blind or stifle the negroes. Pronged stakes were fastened round the throats of the men, and their hands were fixed in blocks of wood nailed together. Boys, of twelve or fourteen years, had their hands only manacled, and the

I could add, were it necessary, a thousand other instances of the scenes of cruelty and bloodshed which are exhibited in Africa, having their origin in the Slave Trade ; but enough has been said to prove the assertion with which I set out, that the principal and almost the only cause of war in the interior of Africa is the desire to procure slaves for traffic; and that the only difference betwixt the former times and the present day is this—that the mortality consequent on the cruelties of the system has increased in proportion to the increase of the traffic, which, it appears, has doubled in amount, as compared with the period antecedent to 1790.

I shall now estimate, as nearly as I can, the probable extent of mortality peculiarly incident to the period of seizure; but the difficulty of this is great, because our authorities on this point are not numerous. Lord Muncaster notices a statement of an African Governor to the Committee of

young children and women were without any incumbrance. Two or three times Almas saw a stubborn slave drawn (to use his expression) like a carriage, by a horse across the rocks, until he was dead. He cannot say how many were killed in the attack; he thinks 500 were taken along with him from Korgo, but many of these died of thirst, hunger, and fatigue, on their march to Kordofan. Almas's father and brother were captured along with him, and the former was compelled to wear the pronged stick from Gebel Noobah to Kordofan. They are both soldiers at Sobeyet. His mother was seized by the sultan of Baggarah, who makes expeditions continually against the inhabitants of Gebel Noobah."

1790:—" Mr. Miles said, he will not admit it to be war, only skirmish-fighting; and yet," Lord Muncaster adds, " Villault, who was on the Gold Coast in 1663, tells us, that in one of these ' skirmishes' above 60,000 men were destroyed; and Bosman says that in two of these ' skirmishes' the outrage was so great, that above 100,000 men were killed upon the spot. Mr. Devaynes also informs us that, while he was in the country, one of these ' skirmishes' happened between the kings of Dahorney and Eyo, in which 60,000 lost their lives."*

The Rev. John Newton, rector of St. Mary's Woolnooth (who at one period of his life was engaged in slave-traffic on the coast of Africa,) observes, " I verily believe that the far greater part of the wars in Africa would cease, if the Europeans would cease to tempt them by offering goods for slaves; and, though they do not bring legions into the field, their wars are bloody. I believe the *captives reserved for sale* are FEWER than *the slain*. I have not sufficient data to warrant calculation, but I suppose that not less than 100,000 slaves are exported annually from all parts of Africa. *If but an equal number* are killed in war, and if many of these wars are kindled by the incentive of selling their prisoners, what an annual accumulation of blood must there be crying against the nations of Europe concerned in this trade!"†

I have no *modern* authority to support the spe-

* Lord Muncaster on the Slave Trade, p. 42.
† Newton on the Slave Trade. London, 1788, p. 30.

cific statements of Newton and Lord Muncaster, excepting that of Denham, who says, "That in one instance *twenty thousand* were *killed,* for *sixteen thousand* carried away into slavery;"[*] and in another case, that " probably *more than double* " the number of those captured for slaves fell a sacrifice in the onset of the captors.[†]

The second head of mortality, arising from the March, and Detention before being embarked, comes next in order; and first as to the

MARCH.

" The Begarmese," says Browne, in his journey to Darfour in 1793, " attack on horseback the Kardee, Serrowa, Showa, Battah, and Mulgui tribes, and, seizing as many captives as possible, drive them like cattle to Begarmi."[‡] Mungo Park informs us that " by far the greater number of slaves purchased by Europeans on the coast are brought down in large caravans from the inland countries, of which many are unknown even by name to the Europeans.

" I was met," he says, " by a coffle (caravan) of slaves, about seventy in number, coming from Sego. They were tied together by their necks, with thongs of bullocks' hide twisted like a rope, seven slaves upon a thong, and a man with a musket between every seven. Many of the slaves were ill-conditioned, and a great number of them women; they

---

[*] Denham's Narrative, p. 214.　　[†] Ibid., p. 116.
[‡] See Leyden's Discoveries, vol. i. p. 413.

were going to Morocco by the way of Ludamar and the Great Desert."*

In another part of his journal, Park says that, on his route to Pisania, (a distance of 500 miles,) he joined a coffle, under a slattee (slave-merchant), Kaarfa, who was particularly kind to him, and whom he describes as "a worthy negro, with a mind above his condition—a good creature," and therefore not likely to be among the most cruel, in the treatment of his slaves. While this slattee was collecting the coffle, Park arrived at his house. Kaarfa liberally offered to keep him there till the country should be fit for travelling. On the third day after his arrival Park fell ill with the fever, and he bestows great praise on his " benevolent landlord," for his kindness and attention.† We are afterwards informed of the treatment of the slaves during the journey, which, be it remembered, was performed under the direction of this " worthy, good, and benevolent negro." It appears that " The slaves are commonly secured by putting the right leg of one and the left of another into the same pair of fetters. By supporting the fetters with a string, they can walk, though very slowly. Every four slaves are likewise fastened together by the neck, with a strong pair of twisted thongs; and in the night an additional pair of fetters is put on their hands, and sometimes a light iron chain passed around their necks."

* Park's Travels, vol. i. pp. 438, 290.
† Ibid., vol. i. p. 388, &c.

" Such of them as evince marks of discontent are
secured in a different manner ; a thick billet of
wood is cut about three feet long, and, a smooth
notch being made upon one side of it, the ancle
of the slave is bolted to the smooth part by means of
a strong iron staple, one prong of which passes on
each side of the ancle. All these fetters and bolts
are made from native iron. In the present ·case
they were put on by the blacksmith as soon as the
slaves arrived from Kancaba, and ·were not taken
off until the morning when the coffle departed for
Gambia."

He goes on to say, " Even to those who accompanied the caravan as a matter of choice, the toil was
immense ; and they travelled sometimes from morning till night without tasting a morsel of food."
And afterwards—" During this day's travel, two
slaves, a woman and a girl, were so much fatigued
that they could not keep up with the coffle. They
were severely whipped and dragged along, until
about three o'clock in the afternoon, when they were
both affected with vomiting, by which it was discovered that they had eaten clay." He then narrates a
case of great cruelty : one of the female slaves had
become quite exhausted, and every exertion was made
by the whip to cause her to keep up with the coffle.
When every effort failed, " the general cry of the
coffle was ' kang-tegi ' (cut her throat). I had not
walked forward a mile, when one of Kaarfa's domestic
slaves came up to me with poor Nealee's garment
upon the end of his bow and exclaimed, ' Nealee

is lost ;' he afterwards said, he had left her on the
road."* A few days after this took place, a party of
Serawoolie traders joined the coffle, and one of their
male slaves became also completely exhausted ; he
was whipped and tortured to no purpose, and then
left in charge of another slave, who, it was generally
believed, put him to death.

It appears that there is also great suffering when
these poor victims are conveyed to the coast, by the
rivers. Falconbridge says, " While I was on the
coast, during one of the voyages I made, the black
traders brought down in different canoes from 1200
to 1500 negroes, which had been purchased at one
fair." They consisted of all ages. Women sometimes form a part of them who happen to be so far
advanced in their pregnancy as to be delivered
during their journey from the fairs to the coast.
And there is not the least room to doubt, but that,
even before they can reach the fairs, great numbers
perish from cruel usage, want of food, travelling
through inhospitable deserts, &c. They are brought
in canoes, at the bottom of which they lie, having
their hands tied, and a strict watch is kept over
them. Their usage, in other respects, during the
passage, is equally cruel. Their allowance of food
is so scanty as barely to support nature. They
are, besides, much exposed to the violent rains which
frequently fall here, being covered only with mats
that afford but a slight defence ; and, as there is

* Park's Travels, vol. i. p. 507, &c.

usually water at the bottom of the canoes, from leaking, they are scarcely ever dry."*

Here, again, it may be rejoined, " But these were the practices of the last century." Riley informs us that Sidi Hamet, the Moor, narrated to him, as an instance of the sufferings consequent on the route by the Desert, that the caravan which he accompanied from Wednoon to Timbuctoo, in 1807, consisted on its setting out of 1000 men and 4000 camels; but only twelve camels and twenty-one men escaped alive from the Desert † Let us examine whether these cruel sufferings have been mitigated in our own times; and whether we may flatter ourselves that Africa is no longer the scene of such atrocities. Burckhardt, in 1814, accompanied a caravan from Shendy in Nubia, across the Desert, to Suakin on the Red Sea. There were slaves with the caravan on their way to Arabia. In the middle of the journey the caravan was alarmed by a threatened attack of robbers; they " moved on," we are told, "in silence; nothing was heard but the groans of a few infirm female slaves, and the whips of their cruel masters."‡ He also says that the females are almost universally the victims of the brutal lusts of their drivers.

Major Gray, while travelling in the country of Galam in 1821, fell in with a part of the Kaartan

* Falconbridge on the Slave Trade. London, 1788, pp. 12, 13, 19, &c.

† Riley's Narrative, p. 361.

‡ Burckhardt's Travels, pp. 381, 336.

force, which he said had taken 107 prisoners, chiefly women and children. "The men were tied in pairs by the necks, their hands secured behind their backs; the women by their necks only, but their hands were not left free from any sense of feeling for them, but in order to enable them to balance the immense loads of pang, corn, or rice, which they were forced to carry on their heads, and the children (who were unable to walk, or sit on horse-back) behind their backs. They were hurried along at a pace little short of running, to enable them to keep up with the horsemen, who drove them on as Smithfield drovers do fatigued bullocks. Many of the women were old, and by no means able to endure such treatment." On a subsequent day he says, "The sufferings of the poor slaves during a march of nearly eight hours, partly under an excessively hot sun and east wind, heavily laden with water, of which they were allowed to drink but very sparingly, and travelling bare foot on a hard and broken soil, covered with long dried reeds, and thorny underwood, may be more easily conceived than described."

In the course of his journey Major Gray fell in with another detachment of slaves, and he says, "The women and children (all nearly naked, and carrying heavy loads) were tied together by the neck, and hurried along over a rough stony path, that cut their feet in a dreadful manner. There were a great number of children, who, from their

tender years, were unable to walk; and were carried, some on the prisoners' backs, and others on
horseback behind the captors, who, to prevent their
falling off, tied them to the back part of the saddle
with a rope made from the bark of the baoball,
which was so hard and rough that it cut the back
and sides of the poor little innocent babes, so as to
draw the blood. This, however, was only a secondary state of the sufferings endured by those children,
when compared to the dreadfully blistered and chafed
state of their seats, from constant jolting on the bare
back of the horse, seldom going slower than a trot,
or smart amble, and not unfrequently driven at full
speed for a few yards, and pulled up short."*

In speaking of the route by the Desert, Lyon
says :†—" Children are thrown with the baggage on
the camels, if unable to walk ; but, if five or six years
of age, the poor little creatures are obliged to trot on
all day, even should no stop be made for fourteen
or fifteen hours, as I have sometimes witnessed."
" The daily allowance of food is a quart of dates
in the morning, and half a pint of flour, made into
bazeen, at night. Some masters never allow their
slaves to drink after a meal, except at a watering-
place." " None of the owners ever moved without
their whips, which were in constant use. Drinking
too much water, bringing too little wood, or falling
asleep before the cooking was finished, were con-

---

* Gray's Travels in Africa, pp. 290, 295, and 323.
† Lyon, p. 297.

sidered nearly capital crimes; and it was in vain for these poor creatures to plead the excuse of being tired,—nothing could avert the application of the whip." "No slave dares to be ill or unable to walk; but, when the poor sufferer dies, the master suspects there must have been something 'wrong inside,' and regrets not having liberally applied the *usual* remedy of burning the belly with a red-hot iron; thus reconciling themselves to their cruel treatment of these unfortunate wretches."

This description is confirmed by Caillie, who, in his account of his journey from Timbuctoo through the Desert, gives the following case of barbarity, which he says he had the misfortune to see too often repeated:—"A poor Bambara slave of twenty-five years was cruelly treated by some Moors, who compelled him to walk, without allowing him to halt for a moment, or to quench his burning thirst. The complaints of this unfortunate creature might have moved the hardest heart. Sometimes he would beg to rest himself against the crupper of a camel; and at others he threw himself down on the sand in despair. In vain did he implore, with uplifted hands, a drop of water; his cruel masters answered his prayers and his tears only with stripes."*

In another part of his work Caillie says—

"Our situation was still the same; the east wind blew with violence; and, far from affording us any

* Caillie's Travels, vol. ii. p. 89.

G

refreshment, it only threatened to bury us under the mountains of sand which it raised ; and, what was still more alarming, our water diminished rapidly from the extreme drought which it occasioned. Nobody suffered more intensely from thirst than the poor little slaves, who were crying for water. Exhausted by their sufferings and their lamentations, these unhappy creatures fell on the ground, and seemed to have no power to rise ; but the Moors did not suffer them to continue there long when travelling. Insensible to the sufferings which childhood is so little fitted to support, these barbarians dragged them along with violence, beating them incessantly till they had overtaken the camels, which were already at a distance."*

In 1824 Denham and Clapperton penetrated to Nigritia by the Desert from Fezzan, the route usually taken by slave-caravans going to the north of Africa. In narrating his excursion to Munga, Major Denham speaks of a caravan which he met at Kouka, consisting of ten merchants from Soudan with nearly 100 slaves, and he observes, " If the hundreds, nay thousands, of skeletons that whiten in the blast between this place and Mourzouk, did not of themselves tell a tale replete with woe, the difference of appearance in all slaves here (where they are fed tolerably), and the state in which they usually arrive in Fezzan, would but too clearly prove the acuteness of the sufferings which commence on their leaving the

* Caillie's Travels, vol. ii. p. 114.

negro country : going as they do, poor creatures, nearly naked, the cold of Fezzan, in the winter season, kills them by hundreds."* This fact, as to the change of climate, is also noticed by Captain Lyon, who, speaking of the passage across the mountains of Fezzan, says, " Feb. 12th, Ther. 30° below 0°.— Water freezes, and the poor negroes in great distress from the cold."†

When the travellers arrived at the well of Meshroo, Denham says : " Round this spot were lying more than one hundred skeletons : our camels did not come up till dark, and we bivouacked in the midst of those unearthed remains of the victims of persecution and avarice, after a long day's journey of twenty-six miles, in the course of which one of our party counted 107 of these skeletons." Shortly afterwards, he adds: " During the last two days we had passed on an average from sixty to eighty or ninety skeletons each day ; but the numbers that lay about the wells at El Hammar were countless."‡ Jackson informs§ us that in 1805 " a caravan from Timbuctoo to Tafilet was disappointed at not finding water at the usual watering-place, and entirely perished ; 2000 persons and 1800 camels."

Dr. Holroyd, in the letter to me which I have already quoted, in speaking of the " gaswah " in Kordofan, says : " These slave-hunts have produced a

* Denham, pp. 172, 280.   † Lyon, p. 298.
‡ Denham, p. 12.
§ Jackson's Travels in Africa, 1809, p. 239.

great depopulation in the districts where they are
practised; there is not only a terrible waste of life in
the attempts to capture the negroes, but after they
are seized there is so much of ill-usage and brutality
that I have been assured that *no less than thirty per
cent. perish* in the first ten days after their seizure."

Dr. Bowring stated to me, that " in conversa-
tions which I have had with the domestic slaves
in the towns of Egypt, they talk with the greatest
horror of the sufferings connected with their first
experience of the bitterness of slavery. And these
are but the beginning of sorrows. In the progress
across the Desert many perish from thirst and from
fatigue. I have often heard their miseries described
on their way, from the poverty of the fellahs and
insufficiency of the caravans, which are often charged
with an excessive number of slaves. An estimate
being made of the greatest number which it is possible to preserve with the supply of water that remains, all the rest are abandoned and die of starvation in the sandy wilderness."

" I will give you from the mouth, and nearly in the
words, of a female slave at Cairo, her account of the
journey across the Desert to Siout. 'We had a
long, long journey, and we suffered very much. We
had not food enough to eat, and sometimes we had
no drink at all, and our thirst was terrible. When
we stopped, almost dying for want of water, they
killed a camel and gave us his blood to drink. But
the camels themselves could not get on, and then

they were killed, and we had their flesh for meat and their blood for water. Some of the people were too weak to get on, and so they were left in the Desert to die. The fellahs were some of them good people, and when we were tired allowed us to ride upon the camels ; but there were many who would never let the negroes ride, but forced them always to walk, always over the sand—but when we had been days without water, many dropped down and were left upon the sand ; so that, when we got to the end of our journey, numbers of those that had been with us were with us no longer.' "

Dr. Holroyd says that " These unfortunate individuals (those selected for the army) were marched down to Kartoom, fourteen days' journey, completely naked ; and, to add to their misery, a wooden stake, six or seven feet long, and forked at one extremity, was attached to the neck of one by means of a cross bar retained in its position by stripes of bull's hide ; to the other end of the stake an iron ring was fastened, which encircled the throat of another of these poor harmless creatures. They were then unmercifully driven to Kartoom, with scarcely anything to eat on the way, and compelled to traverse a burning desert with a very sparing and scanty supply of water. They were dispatched in companies of fifties, and so great were their privations and fatigue on the journey, that a letter arrived at Kordofan, addressed to Mustapha Bey, from Shorshid Pacha, of Kartoom, Governor General of Soudan, and which was read during a visit I made to the divan of the former, in which the latter stated, that of fifty slaves who left Kordofan some days before, only thirty-five were living on the arrival of the caravan at Kartoom.

Richard Lander, in his account of Captain Clapperton's last journey in 1826, in which he attended that traveller, speaking of the state of the slaves whom he saw on their journeys, observes: "In their toilsome journeyings from one part of the country to another, it must be admitted that the captured slaves undergo incredible hardships." He left Socatoo, with a party of traders, and the "king of Jacoba," who had fifty slaves, whom he was conducting (with heavy loads on their heads) to his own country. Two days afterwards Lander was informed that the whole of these slaves were missing; and on search being made, it was ascertained that they *had all perished from excessive fatigue and want of water.**

Mr. Oldfield, who accompanied Laird in the expedition up the Niger in 1833, in giving a description of Bocqua market, says: " Under the mats and in the enclosures, are to be seen male and female slaves from the age of five, up to thirty. Some of these children of misfortune, more intelligent than others, are to be seen sitting pensive and melancholy, apparently in deep thought, while their poor legs are swelled from confinement in irons, or being closely stowed at the bottom of a canoe ; and he adds, " It is painful to contemplate the number of slaves annually

* Lander's Records, vol. i. p. 301; and vol. ii. p. 95.

sold at this market, most of whom are forwarded to the sea-side."*

Many more extracts might have been taken, from the remarks of modern travellers, on this branch of the subject; but enough has been adduced to prove that the cruelties and consequent mortality arising from *the march after seizure* have not *decreased* since the time of Falconbridge and Park.

I shall only further add, on the authority of Dr. Meyen, (a German who, a few years ago, published an account of a Voyage round the World,) that " M. Mendez, the author of a very learned treatise on the Causes of the great Mortality of the Negro Slaves, estimates the number of those who die, merely on the journey from the interior to the coast, *at five-twelfths of the whole.*"†

DETENTION.

The next cause of mortality arises from the detention of the slaves on the coast, before they are embarked, and this occurs, for the most part, when the vessel for which they may be destined, has not arrived, or is not ready to sail, or may be in dread of capture after sailing.

A gentleman resident at Senegal in 1818, stated to his correspondent at Paris, that, " No one in the town is ignorant that there are here 600 wretched creatures shut up in the slave yards, waiting for

* Laird and Oldfield, vol. i. p. 409.
† Dr. Meyen, German edition, vol. i. p. 77.

embarkation. The delay which has occurred causing
a serious expense, they receive only what is sufficient
to keep them alive, and they are made to go out for a
short space of time, morning and evening, loaded
with irons.*

When Commodore Owen visited Benguela in
1825, he says, " We had here an opportunity of seeing bond slaves of both sexes chained together in
pairs. About 100 of these unhappy beings had just
arrived from a great distance in the interior. Many
were mere skeletons labouring under every misery
that want and fatigue could produce. In some, the
fetters had, by their constant action, worn through
the lacerated flesh to the bare bone, the ulcerated
wound having become the resort of myriads of flies,
which had deposited their eggs in the gangrenous
cavities."†

Oiseau, commanding the brig Le Louis, on completing his cargo of slaves at the Old Calebar, thrust
the whole of the unfortunate beings between decks,
a height of nearly three feet, and closed the hatches
for the night. When morning made its appearance,
fifty of the poor sufferers had paid the debt of nature.
The wretch coolly ordered the bodies of his victims
to be thrown into the river, and immediately proceeded
on shore to complete his execrable cargo.‡

Richard Lander tells us that the Brazen, in which
he went to Africa in 1825, captured a Spanish bri-

---

* 13th Report of the African Institution, Ap. G. p. 99.
† Owen, vol. ii. p. 234.   ‡ Class B. 1825, p. 123.

gantine which was waiting off Accra, for a cargo of slaves. A few days after this capture, the commander of the Brazen landed at Papoe, and demanded the slaves which were to have been embarked in the brigantine. They were ultimately given up, and Lander says, "The slaves at length made their appearance, and exhibited a long line of melancholy faces, and emaciated frames, wasted by disease and close confinement, and by their having suffered dreadfully from scantiness of food, and the impure air of their prison-house. They were in a complete state of nudity, and heavily manacled; several of them were lamed by the weight of their irons, and their skin sadly excoriated from the same cause.*

At the close of this journey, Lander says:—" I saw 400 slaves at Badagry in the Bight of Benin, crammed into a small schooner of eighty tons. The appearance of these unhappy human beings was squalid and miserable in the extreme; they were fastened by the neck in pairs, only one-fourth of a yard of chain being allowed for each, and driven to the beach by a parcel of hired scoundrels, whilst their associates in cruelty were in front of the party pulling them along by a narrow band, their only apparel, which encircled the waist." "Badagry being a general mart for the sale of slaves to European merchants, it not unfrequently happens that the market is either overstocked with human beings, or no buyers are to be

* Lander's Records, vol. i. p. 31.

found; in which case the maintenance of the unhappy slaves devolves solely on the Government.
The king then causes an examination to be made,
when the sickly, as well as the old and infirm, are
carefully selected and chained by themselves in one
of the factories (five of which, containing upwards
of one thousand slaves of both sexes, were at Badagry
during my residence there); and next day the
majority of these poor wretches are pinioned and
conveyed to the banks of the river, where having
arrived, a weight of some sort is appended to their
necks, and being rowed in canoes to the middle of
the stream, they are flung into the water, and left
to perish by the pitiless Badagrians. Slaves, who
for other reasons are rejected by the merchants,
undergo the same punishment, or are left to endure
more lively torture at the sacrifices, by which means
hundreds of human beings are annually destroyed."*

Mr. Leonard informs us, "that about 1830, the
king of Loango told the officers of the Primrose that
he could load eight slave-vessels in one week, and
give each 400 or 500; but that, having now no means
of disposing of the greater part of his prisoners, he
was obliged to kill them. And, shortly before the
Primrose arrived, a great number of unfortunate
wretches, who had been taken in a predatory incur-
sion, after having been made use of to carry loads
of the plundered ivory, &c., to the coast, on their
arrival there, as there was no market for them, and

* Lander's Records, vol. ii pp. 241, 250.

as the trouble and expense of their support would be considerable, they were taken to the side of a hill, a little beyond the town, and coolly knocked on the head."*

In 1833 Mr. Oldfield found several dozen human skulls lining the bank of the river Nunn, (one of the mouths of the Niger,) at a barracoon or slave-house, which he discovered were the remains of slaves who had died there.†

An intelligent master of a merchant-vessel, who, for many years past, has been engaged in the African trade, informs me, that after the slave-dealing captains have made their selection of the slaves brought on board for sale, the unfortunate creatures who may be rejected "are sent immediately on shore, and marched down to the barracoon, chained together, a distance of five miles. I have seen the most piteous entreaties made by the poor rejected creatures to the captain to take them, for they knew that to be returned on shore was only to encounter a worse fate by starvation." He is speaking of the River Bonny, and he goes on to say, " Ju Ju town contains about twelve barracoons : they are built to contain from 300 to 700 slaves each. I have seen from 1500 to 2000 slaves at a time, belonging to the several vessels then in the river."

" I have known disease to make dreadful havoc in these places, more especially in the year 1831,

---

* Leonard's Voyage to Western Africa, p. 147.
† Laird and Oldfield's Journal, vol. i. p. 339.

when the small-pox carried off 200 in one barracoon. Great numbers are carried off annually by diarrhœa and other diseases."

Colonel Nicolls has stated to me that, during his residence at Fernando Po, he visited the River Cameroons, where he saw a number of slaves in a barracoon; " they were confined in irons, two and two, and many of them had the irons literally grating against their bones through the raw flesh."

It is stated by a naval officer serving in the Preventive Squadron, in a letter to a relative, dated about a year ago, and communicated to me, that in 1837, having been employed in blockading a Portuguese brig, up one of the rivers in the Bight of Biafra, " On arriving at my station, I had positive information that the Portuguese had bought upwards of 400 slaves, and was about to sail. By some means or other, she got information that a British boat was blockading her, consequently she postponed her sailing for several weeks. Shortly afterwards, on my inquiring into her state, I found 300 of her slaves had died chiefly of starvation, and a few were shot by the Portuguese whilst attempting to escape. A few days afterwards the brig sailed without any slaves, all with the exception of about a score, having fallen victims to the system pursued."

Captain Cook has informed me that he saw many blind negroes in Quilimane (1837), who subsisted by begging; they were the remains, he was informed, of a cargo landed from a Monte Videan vessel, which had been attacked by ophthalmia. If they lived, they were left to starve.

He also says, that in September, 1837, a number of slaves were suffocated on board the brig Generous at Quilimane. " The boatswain had, it appeared, shut the hatches close down after the slaves had been put below in the evening; it was his duty to have kept the hatch uncovered, and to have placed guards over them; but this would have required his own vigilance, and he considered a sound sleep was to him worth all the slaves on board, especially as they cost him nothing." This case came to Captain Cook's knowledge in consequence of a quarrel between the captain and the boatswain. " The pecuniary loss was all that was regretted by the captain."

Captain Cook adds, that slaves who " die on board, in port, are never interred on shore, but are invariably thrown overboard, when they sometimes float backward and forward with the tide for a week, should the sharks and alligators not devour them. Should a corpse chance to be washed on shore at the top of high-water, it is permitted to remain until the vultures dispose of it." " I have known one to be near the Custom-house upwards of a week, during which time the stench was intolerable."

In a letter addressed by Captain Cook to the editor of the Standard, dated 16th July 1838, he says that instances have been known of slaves having been buried alive in Quilimane for some trifling

offence, and that the consequent punishment (if there
was any at all) was a mere trifle, as imprisonment
for a month ; and he adds,—

" The fact, however, which I am now about to
state, occurred in August, 1837, and came under my
own observation, and to all of which I am ready to
bear testimony on oath, if required. Slaves to the
number of 250, or thereabouts, male and female,
adults and children, were brought in canoes from
Senna, a Portuguese settlement at some distance in
the interior of Africa, to be sold at Quilimane, there
being at that time several slavers lying in the river.
These unfortunate beings were consigned to a
person holding a high civil appointment under the
Portuguese Government (the collector of customs):
these poor creatures were from a part of the country
where it is said that the natives make bad slaves ;
consequently, and as there was abundance of human
flesh in the market, they did not meet with a ready
sale. The wretch to whom they were consigned
actually refused them sustenance of any kind. Often
have I been compelled to witness the melancholy
spectacle of from twelve to twenty of my fellow-
creatures, without distinction of age or sex, chained
together, with a heavy iron chain round the neck,
wandering about the town in quest of food to satisfy
the cravings of nature, picking up bones and garbage
of every description from the dung-heaps, snails from
the fields, and frogs from the ditches, and, when the
tide receded, collecting the shell-fish that were left

on the bank of the river, or sitting round a fire roasting and eagerly devouring the sea-weed.

" Again and again have I seen one or more of these poor creatures, when unable from sickness to walk, crawling on their hands and knees, accompanying the gang to which they were chained when they went in search of their daily food .... for one could not move without the whole. In consequence of this treatment, they soon became so emaciated that the slave-dealers would not purchase them on any terms ; in this state, horrid as it must appear, the greater part were left to perish, without food, medicine, or clothing, for the little piece of coarse cotton cloth, worn by a few of the females, did not deserve the name, and could answer no other purpose than to lodge the vermin with which they were covered ; their bones protruding through the skin, they presented the appearance of living skeletons, lingering amidst hunger and disease till death, their best friend, released most of them at once, from suffering and bondage."

From these extracts, it is evident that this branch of the case furnishes an item of no small magnitude in the black catalogue of negro destruction.

I now proceed to the

MIDDLE PASSAGE.

" The stings of a wounded conscience, man cannot inflict ; but
nearly all which man can do to make his fellow-creatures miserable,
without defeating his purpose by putting a speedy end to their existence, will still be here effected : and it will still continue true,
that never can so much misery be found condensed into so small a
space as in a slave-ship during the middle passage "—*Wilberforce,*
Letter, 1807.

It was well observed by Mr. Fox, in a debate on
the Slave Trade, that " True humanity consists not
in a squeamish ear ; it consists not in starting or
shrinking at such tales as these, but in a disposition
of heart to relieve misery. True humanity apper-
tains rather to the mind than to the nerves, and
prompts men to use real and active endeavours to
execute the actions which it suggests."

In the spirit of this observation, I now go on to
remark, that the first feature of this deadly passage,
which attracts our attention, is the evident insufficiency, in point of tonnage, of the vessels employed,
for the cargoes of human beings which they are made
to contain.

In 1788 a law passed the British legislature, by
which it was provided that vessels under 150 tons
should not carry more than five men to every three
tons ; that vessels above 150 tons should not carry
more than three men to every two tons ; and that
the height of slave-vessels between decks should
not be less than five feet. In 1813 it was decreed

by the government of Portugal and Brazil that two tons should be allowed for every five men ; and the Spanish " Cedula," of 1817, adopted the same scale. It is understood that the Spanish and Portuguese ton bears the proportion of one and a half to the British ton. The allowance in British transports is three men to every two tons.

	Men.	Tons.
The lowest rate then allowed by the British was . . .	5 to	3
And by Spain, Portugal, and Brazil, it should be	5 to	3
But for British soldiers the regulation is	3 to	2

and, although this allowance in the transport of troops seems to be liberal, when compared with the space afforded for slaves, even here complaints have often been made of the insufficiency.

Let us then keep in view these rates of tonnage, as we proceed to ascertain the accommodation which has been, and is now, afforded to the negroes on the middle passage ; and here, at least, one reason will be apparent for the increase of suffering and mortality which have recently occurred, viz. that the extent of accommodation, limited as it was, has been *greatly curtailed.*

We have a faithful description of the miseries of the middle passage, from the pen of an eye-witness, Mr. Falconbridge. His account refers to a period antecedent to 1790. He tells us, that " The men

H

negroes, on being brought aboard ship, are immediately
fastened together two and two, by handcuffs on their
wrists, and by irons riveted on their legs." "They
are frequently stowed so close as to admit of no
other posture than lying on their sides. Neither will
the height between decks, unless directly under the
grating, permit them the indulgence of an erect posture, especially where there are platforms, which is
generally the case. These platforms are a kind of
shelf, about eight or nine feet in breadth, extending
from the side of the ship towards the centre. They
are placed nearly midway between the decks at the
distance of two or three feet from each deck. Upon
these the negroes are stowed in the same manner as
they are on the deck underneath." After mentioning some other arrangements, he goes on to say, " It
often happens that those who are placed at a distance
from the buckets, in endeavouring to get to them,
tumble over their companions, in consequence of their
being shackled. These accidents, although unavoid-
able, are productive of continual quarrels, in which
some of them are always bruised. In this distressed
situation they desist from the attempt, and . . . .
This becomes a fresh source of broils and disturbances.
and tends to render the situation of the poor captive
wretches still more uncomfortable."

" In favourable weather they are fed upon deck,
but in bad weather their food is given to them below.
Numberless quarrels take place among them during
their meals ; more especially when they are put upon

short allowance, which frequently happens. In that case, the weak are obliged to be content with a very scanty portion. Their allowance of water is about half a pint each, at every meal.

" Upon the negroes refusing to take sustenance, I have seen coals of fire, glowing hot, put on a shovel, and placed so near their lips as to scorch and burn them, and this has been accompanied with threats of forcing them to swallow the coals, if they any longer persisted in refusing to eat. These means have generally the desired effect. I have also been credibly informed that a certain captain in the Slave Trade poured melted lead on such of the negroes as obstinately refused their food." Falconbridge then tells us that the negroes are sometimes compelled to dance and to sing, and that, if any reluctance is exhibited, the cat-o'-nine-tails is employed to enforce obedience. He goes on to mention the unbounded licence given to the officers and crew of the slavers, as regards the women; and, speaking of the officers, he says, they " are sometimes guilty of such brutal excesses as disgrace human nature." " But," he continues, " the hardships and inconveniences suffered by the negroes during the passage are scarcely to be enumerated or conceived. They are far more violently affected by the sea-sickness than the Europeans. It frequently terminates in death, especially among the women. The exclusion of the fresh air is among the most intolerable. Most ships have air-ports; but, whenever the sea is rough and the rain heavy, it be-

comes necessary to shut these and every other conveyance by which air is admitted. The fresh air
being thus excluded, the negroes' rooms very soon
grow intolerably hot. The confined air, rendered
noxious by the effluvia exhaled from their bodies,
and by being repeatedly breathed, soon produces
fevers and fluxes, which generally carry off great
numbers of them. During the voyages I made I
was frequently a witness to the fatal effects of this
exclusion of the fresh air. I will give one instance,
as it serves to convey some idea, though a very faint
one,* of the state of these unhappy beings. Some
wet and blowing weather having occasioned the
port-holes to be shut, and the gratings to be covered,
fluxes and fevers among the negroes ensued. My pro-
fession requiring it, I frequently went down among
them, till at length their apartments became so extremely hot, as to be only sufferable for a very short
time. But the excessive heat was not the only thing
that rendered their situation intolerable. The deck,
that is, the floor of their rooms, was so covered with

---

* One circumstance has struck me very forcibly. I have received communications, both by letter and in conversation, from
many naval officers who have boarded slave-ships, and I have
observed, that without an exception they all make this observation—" No words can describe the horrors of the scene, or the
sufferings of the negroes." I have recently shown these pages
to a naval officer, now a Captain in the service, who had long been
employed in the preventive squadron, requesting him to point out
any error into which I might have fallen. He replied, " Your
statement is true as far as it goes; but it is, after all, only a
faint picture of the reality."

the blood and mucus which had proceeded from them in consequence of the flux, that it resembled a slaughter-house. It is not in the power of the human imagination to picture to itself a situation more dreadful or more disgusting.

" Numbers of the slaves having fainted, they were carried on deck, where several of them died; and the rest were with great difficulty restored. It had nearly proved fatal to me also; the climate was too warm to admit the wearing of any clothing but a shirt, and that I had pulled off before I went down; notwithstanding which, by only continuing among them for about a quarter of an hour, I was so overcome by the heat, stench, and foul air, that I had nearly fainted; and it was not without assistance that I could get upon deck. The consequence was, that I soon after fell sick of the same disorder, from which I did not recover for several months. A circumstance of this kind sometimes repeatedly happens in the course of a voyage, and often to a greater degree than what has just been described; particularly when the slaves are much crowded, which was not the case at that time, the ship having more than 100 short of the number she was to have taken in; yet, out of 380, 105 died on the passage,—a proportion seemingly very great, but by no means uncommon."

He proceeds to notice the case of a Liverpool vessel, which took on board at the Bonny River nearly 700 slaves (more than three to each ton !) ;

and Falconbridge says,—" By purchasing so great
a number, the slaves were so crowded, that they
were even obliged to lie one upon another. This
occasioned such a mortality among them, that, without meeting with unusual bad weather, or having a
longer voyage than common, nearly one-half of them
died before the ship arrived in the West Indies."
He then describes the treatment of the sick as
follows :—" The place allotted for the sick negroes
is under the half-deck, where they lie on the bare
plank. By this means, those who are emaciated
frequently have their skin, and even their flesh, entirely rubbed off, by the motion of the ship, from the
prominent parts of the shoulders, elbows, and hips,
so as to render the bones in those parts quite bare.
The excruciating pain which the poor sufferers feel
from being obliged to continue in so dreadful a situation, frequently, for several weeks, in case they
happen to live so long, is not to be conceived or
described. Few indeed are ever able to withstand
the fatal effects of it. The surgeon, upon going
between decks in the morning, frequently finds several of the slaves dead, and, among the men, sometimes a dead and a living negro fastened by their
irons together."

He then states that surgeons are driven to engage
in the " Guinea Trade" by the confined state of their
finances ; and that at most the only way in which a
surgeon can render himself useful is by seeing that
the food is properly cooked and distributed to the

slaves : " when once the fever and dysentery get to any height at sea, a cure is scarcely ever effected." " One-half, sometimes two-thirds, and even beyond that, have been known to perish. Before we left Bonny River no less than fifteen died of fevers and dysenteries, occasioned by their confinement."* Falconbridge also told the Committee of 1790, that, " in stowing the slaves, they wedge them in, so that they had not as much room as a man in his coffin ; that, when going from one side of their rooms to the other, he always took off his shoes, but could not avoid pinching them, and that he had the marks on his feet where they bit and scratched him ; their confinement in this situation was so injurious, that he has known them to go down apparently in good health at night, and found dead in the morning."

Any comment on the statement of Falconbridge must be superfluous; he had been a surgeon in slave-ships, he was a respectable witness before the Committee of Inquiry in 1790, and gave the substance of this statement in evidence. And it ought to be borne in mind that he was an eye-witness of the scenes which he has described. His evidence is the more valuable, when it is considered that we have long been debarred from testimony equally credible and direct; as, since 1807, Britain has taken no part in the slave-traffic ; and it has been the policy of the foreign nations who have continued the trade to conceal, as far as they could, the horrors and miseries which are its attendants.

* Falconbridge, p. 19, &c.

Mr. Granville Sharpe (the zealous advocate of the negro) brought forward a case which aroused public attention to the horrors of this passage. In his Memoirs we have the following account taken from his private memoranda.

" March 19, 1783. Gustavus Vasa called on me with an account of 130 negroes being thrown alive into the sea, from on board an English slave-ship.

" The circumstances of this case could not fail to excite a deep interest. The master of a slave-ship, trading from Africa to Jamaica, and having 440 slaves on board, had thought fit, on a pretext that he might be distressed on his voyage for want of water, to lessen the consumption of it in the vessel, by throwing overboard 132 of the most sickly among the slaves. On his return to England the owners of the ship claimed from the insurers the full value of those drowned slaves, on the ground that there was an absolute necessity for throwing them into the sea, in order to save the remaining crew, and the ship itself. The underwriters contested the existence of the alleged necessity; or, if it had existed, attributed it to the ignorance and improper conduct of the master of the vessel. " This contest of pecuniary interest brought to light a scene of horrid brutality which had been acted during the execution of a detestable plot. From the trial it appeared that the ship Zong, Luke Collingwood master, sailed from the island of St. Thomas, on the coast of Africa, September 6, 1781, with 440 slaves and fourteen whites on board, for Jamaica,

and that in the November following she fell in with
that island ; but, instead of proceeding to some port,
the master, mistaking, as he alleges, Jamaica for
Hispaniola, run her to leeward.   Sickness and mortality had by this time taken place on board the
crowded vessel ; so that, between the time of leaving
the coast of Africa and the 29th of November, sixty
slaves and seven white people had died ; and a great
number of the surviving slaves were then sick and
not likely to live. On that day the master of the
ship called together a few of the officers, and stated
to them that, if the sick slaves died a natural death,
the loss would fall on the owners of the ship ; but, if
they were thrown alive into the sea on any sufficient
pretext of necessity for the safety of the ship, it
would be the loss of the underwriters, alleging, at
the same time, that it would be less cruel to throw
sick wretches into the sea than to suffer them to
linger out a few days under the disorder with which
they were afflicted.

   " To this inhuman proposal the mate, James Kel-
sal, at first objected ; but Collingwood at length prevailed on the crew to listen to it.   He then chose out
from the cargo 132 slaves, and brought them on deck,
all or most of whom were sickly and not likely to
recover, and he ordered the crew by turns to throw
them into the sea.   ' A parcel ' of them were accordingly thrown overboard, and, on counting over the
remainder the next morning, it appeared that the
number so drowned had been fifty-four.   He then

ordered another parcel to be thrown over, which, on a second counting on the succeeding day, was proved to have amounted to forty-two.

" On the third day the remaining thirty-six were brought on deck, and, as these now resisted the cruel purpose of their masters, the arms of twenty-six were fettered with irons, and the savage crew proceeded with the diabolical work, casting them down to join their comrades of the former days. Outraged misery could endure no longer ; the ten last victims sprang disdainfully from the grasp of their tyrants, defied their power, and leaping into the sea, felt a momentary triumph in the embrace of death." *

The evidence taken before the Parliamentary Committees of 1790 and 1791, abounds with similar cases of enormity. I should be entitled, if it were necessary, to quote every one of them, because the middle passage, at that time, when the traffic was legal, was less horrible than now, when it is contraband. But I have limited myself to two extracts; the one, because it is the narrative of a surgeon,† a class of officers now scarcely to be met with in a slave-ship, and because it gives, in a brief and continuous narrative, the chief features of the voyage across the

---

* " Memoirs of Granville Sharp," edited by Prince Hoare London, 1820, pp. 236—238.

† Captain Cook, from whose communication to me I have already given extracts, narrating some of the cruelties of the middle passage, says, " With all this probability, or rather certainty, of disease, I never knew but one slaver that carried a surgeon."

Atlantic; the other, because every fact was proved in a court of justice.

Such were some of the cruelties of the middle passage towards the end of the last century; and it might have been expected, that since that time, some improvement should have taken place; but it is not so: the treatment of slaves by the British, subsequent to the Slave Regulation Act, and down to 1808, was mildness itself, when compared with the miseries consequent on the trade, and the system which has been pursued in the vain attempt to put it down, since that period to the present time.

Mr. Wilberforce, in his letter to his constituents in 1807, observes, " Many of the sufferings of these wretched beings are of a sort for which no legislative regulations can provide a remedy. Several of them, indeed, arise necessarily out of their peculiar circumstances, as connected with their condition on shipboard. It is necessary to the safety of the vessel to secure the men by chains and fetters. It is necessary to confine them below during the night, and in very stormy weather during the day also. Often it happens, that with the numbers still allowed to be taken, especially when some of those epidemic diseases prevail, which, though less frequent than formerly, will yet occasionally happen ; and when men of different countries and languages, or of opposite tempers, are linked together, that such scenes take place as are too nauseous for description. Still in rough weather their limbs must be excoriated by lying

on the boards ; still they will often be wounded
by the fetters; still food and exercise will be deemed
necessary to present the animal in good condition at
the place of sale ; still some of them will loathe their
food, and be averse to exercise, from the joint effect,
perhaps, of sea-sickness and mental uneasiness ; and
still, while in this state, they will probably be charged
with sulkiness ; and eating and dancing in their fetters
will be enforced by stripes ; still, the high netting
will be necessary, that standing precaution of an
African ship against acts of suicide ; but more than
all, still must the diseases of the mind remain entire,
nay, they may perhaps increase in force, from the
attention being less called off by the urgency of
bodily suffering ; the anguish of husbands torn from
their wives,—wives from their husbands, and parents
from their children ; the pangs arising from the consideration that they are separated for ever from their
country, their friends, their relations, and connexions,
remain the same."*

Such is the statement of Wilberforce as to the
middle passage in its mildest form.   This truly great
man had the satisfaction shortly afterwards to witness
the abolition of the traffic on the part of Britain,—a
triumph on the side of humanity, which his unceasing
and strenuous efforts were mainly instrumental in
obtaining.

Since 1808 the English Government has, with
various success, been indefatigably engaged in en-

* Wilberforce's Letter, p. 99, &c.

deavouring to procure the co-operation of foreign powers for the suppression of the Slave Trade. In virtue of the treaties which have been entered into, many vessels engaged in the traffic have been captured ; and much information has been obtained, which has been regularly laid before Parliament. A few of the cases which have been detailed, will now be noticed, for the purpose of ascertaining whether the miseries which have been narrated have ceased to exist ; or whether they do not *now* exist in a more intense degree than at any former period.

The first case I notice is that of the Spanish brig Carlos, captured in 1814. In this vessel of 200 tons, 512 negroes had been put on board (nearly 180 *more* than the complement allowed on the proportion of five slaves to three tons). The captor reported that " they were so miserably fed, clothed, &c., that any idea of the horrors of the Slave Trade would fall short of what I saw. Eighty were thrown overboard before we captured her. In many instances I saw the bones coming through the skin from starvation."*

In the same year (1814) the schooner Aglae, of 40 tons, was captured with a cargo of 152 negroes (nearly four to each ton). " The only care seemed to have been to pack them as close as possible, and tarpaulin was placed over tarpaulin, in order to give the vessel the appearance of being laden with a well-stowed cargo of cotton and rice."†

* African Institution Report, 1815, p. 17.
† Ib., Appendix, p. 86.

In 1815 a lieutenant of the navy thus describes the state of a Portuguese slaver, the St. Joachim : he says, " That within twenty-two days after the vessel had left Mosambique, thirteen of the slaves had died ; that between the capture and their arrival at Simon's Bay, the survivors of them were all sickly and weak, and ninety-two of them afflicted with the flux ; that the slaves were all stowed together, perfectly naked, and nothing but rough, unplaned planks to crouch down upon, in a hold situated over their water and provisions, the place being little more than two feet in height, and the space allowed for each slave so small, that it was impossible for them to avoid touching and pressing upon those immediately surrounding. The greater part of them were fastened, some three together, by one leg, each in heavy iron shackles, a very large proportion of them having the flux. Thus they were compelled," &c. (here a scene of disgusting wretchedness is described). " The pilot being asked by Captain Baker how many he supposed would have reached their destination, replied, ' about half the number that were embarked.'"*

We have next the case of the Rodeur, as stated in a periodical work, devoted to medical subjects, and published at Paris. This vessel, it appears, was of 200 tons' burden. She took on board a cargo of 160 negroes, and after having been fifteen days on her voyage, it was remarked that the slaves had contracted a considerable redness of the eyes, which spread with singular rapidity. At this time they

* Afr. Inst. Report, 1818, p. 27.

were limited to eight ounces of water a-day, for each
person, which quantity was afterwards reduced to
the half of a wine-glass.   By the advice of the surgeon, the slaves who were in the hold were
brought upon deck for the advantage of fresh air;
but it became necessary to abandon this expedient,
as many of them who were affected with nostalgia
threw themselves into the sea, locked in each other's
arms.   The ophthalmia which had spread so rapidly
and frightfully among the Africans, soon began to
infect all on board, and to create alarm for the crew.
The danger of infection, and perhaps the cause
which produced the disease, were increased by a
violent dysentery, attributed to the use of rain-water.
The number of the blind augmented every day.
The vessel reached Guadaloupe on June 21, 1819,
her crew being in a most deplorable condition.
Three days after her arrival, the only man who
during the voyage had withstood the influence of
the contagion, and whom Providence appeared to
have preserved as a guide to his unfortunate companions, was seized with the same malady.   Of the
negroes, thirty-nine had become perfectly blind,
twelve had lost one eye, and fourteen were affected
with blemishes more or less considerable.

   This case excited great interest, and several additional circumstances connected with it were given
to the public.   It was stated that the captain caused
several of the negroes who were prevented in the
attempt to throw themselves overboard, to be shot

and hung, in the hope that the example might deter
the rest from a similar conduct. It is further stated,
that upwards of thirty of the slaves who became
blind were thrown into the sea and drowned, upon
the principle that had they been landed at Guadaloupe, no one would have bought them, while by
throwing them overboard, the expense of maintaining them was avoided, while a ground was laid for
a claim on the underwriters by whom the cargo had
been insured, and who are said to have allowed the
claim, and made good the value of the slaves thus
destroyed.

What more need be said in illustration of the extremity of suffering, induced by the middle passage,
as demonstrated by the case of the Rodeur? But
the supplement must not be omitted. At the time
when only one man could see to steer that vessel,
a large ship approached, "which appeared to be
totally at the mercy of the wind and the waves.
The crew of this vessel, hearing the voices of the
crew of the Rodeur, cried out most vehemently for
help. They told the melancholy tale as they passed
along; that their ship was a Spanish slave-ship, the
St. Leon; and that a contagion had seized the
eyes of all on board, so that there was not one individual sailor or slave who could see. But alas! this
pitiable narrative was in vain; for no help could be
given. The St. Leon passed on, and was never
more heard of!"*

* Afr. Inst. Report, 1820, p. 7.

In the African Institution Report for 1820, I find the following case stated. Captain Kelly, of H.M.S. ship Pheasant, captured on July 30, 1819, a Portuguese schooner, called the Novo Felicidade, belonging to Prince's Island, having on board seventy-one slaves, and a crew, consisting of one master and ten sailors. This vessel measured only eleven tons. She was carried by Captain Kelly to Sierra Leone, for adjudication, and his judicial declaration contains the following statement :—

"I do further declare, that the state in which these unfortunate creatures were found is shocking to every principle of humanity ;—seventeen men shackled together in pairs by the legs, and twenty boys, one on the other, in the main hold,—a space measuring eighteen feet in length, seven feet eight inches main breadth, and one foot eight inches in height; and under them the yams for their support."

The appearance of the slaves, when released from their irons, was most distressing ; scarcely any of them could · stand on their legs, from cramp and evident starvation. The space allowed for the females, thirty-four in number, was even more contracted than that for the men, measuring only nine feet four inches in length, four feet eight inches main breadth, and two feet seven inches in height, but not being confined in irons, and perhaps allowed during the day to come on deck, they did not present so distressing an appearance as the men."*

* Afr. Inst. Report, 1820, p. 11.

I

We have next another instance of the varied cruelties of this part of the subject. La Jeune Estelle captured by Admiral Collier in 1820, after a chase of some hours, during which several casks were observed to be floating in the sea; but no person could be spared at the time to examine them. On boarding the Estelle, the captain denied that he had any slaves on board; but from the very suspicious appearances around, the officer ordered a strict search to be made. An English sailor, on striking a cask, heard a faint voice issue from it, as if of some creature expiring. The cask was immediately opened, when two slave girls, about twelve or fourteen years of age, were found packed up in it; a prisoner on board the captor's ship recognised the girls as two out of fourteen, whom the slaver had carried off from a village on the coast. Admiral Collier, on this, ordered another search to be made, in hopes of discovering the other twelve; but they were nowhere to be found. The painful suspicion then arose that the slaver had packed up the twelve girls in casks, and had thrown them overboard during the chase; but it was too late to ascertain the truth of this conjecture, as the chase had led the English frigate many leagues to leeward of the place where they had observed casks floating in the sea.*

Some of the following extracts are also taken from the Reports of the African Institution :—

* Afr. Inst. Report, 1821, p. 15.

A Spanish schooner, the Vicua, when taken possession of, in 1822, had a lighted match hanging over the open magazine hatch. The match had been placed there by the crew before they escaped. It was seen by one of the British seamen, who boldly put his hat under the burning wick, and removed it. The magazine contained a large quantity of powder. One spark would have blown up 325 unfortunate victims, lying in irons in the hold. These monsters in iniquity expressed their deep regret, after the action, that their diabolical plan had failed. Thumbscrews were also found in this vessel. From confinement and suffering the slaves often injured themselves by beating, and vented their grief upon such as were next them, by biting and tearing their flesh.*

Les Deux Sœurs was of forty-one tons; the Eleanor of about sixty; the first had crammed 132 negroes, the last 135, into a space capable of containing about thirty, at full length.†

In the Report of 1823, we have an account of a gallant feat achieved by the boats of a man-of-war, commanded by Lieutenant Mildmay, on the 15th of April, 1822. The action took place in the river Bonny. On the one side were six sail of slavers, three of which opened a heavy fire upon "the English boats as they advanced. When the latter were near enough for their shots to take effect, the firing was

* Afr. Inst. Report, 1823, p. 29.　　† Ib., 1826, p. 55.

returned. They advanced, and in a short time took possession of all the vessels.

" Many of the slaves jumped overboard during the engagement, and were devoured by the sharks. On board the Yeanam, the slaves suffered much; four were killed, and ten wounded. Of the wounded, three were females ; one girl, of about ten years old, lost both her legs, another her right arm, and a third was shot in the side. Even after the vessel had been surrendered, a number of the Spanish sailors skulked below, and, arming the slaves with muskets, made them fire upwards on the British. On board this ship Lieutenant Mildmay observed a slave girl, about twelve or thirteen years of age, in irons, to which was fastened a thick iron chain, ten feet in length, that was dragged along as she moved."*

Commodore Bullen writes, of date September 5, 1825, that the Brazen, last October, overtook L'Eclair. " She belongs to Nantz. The master stated that he had lost a third of his cargo in embarking them. She measured three feet one inch between decks ; the men chained ; many of them unable to sit upright."†

A resident at Freetown thus writes in the Sierra Leone Gazette of the 11th of December, 1823 :— " Having gone off to the slave-vessels lately sent into this harbour, I was struck by the appearance of some very fierce dogs, of the bloodhound species, natives

* Afr. Inst. Report, 1823, p. 28.   † Ib., 1826, p. 60.

of Brazil, and, on inquiry, found that they had been
taken on board for the purpose of assisting their inhuman masters in coercing the unfortunate victims
of their lawless cupidity. They had been trained, it
appears, to sit watch over the hatches during the
night, or whenever the wretched beings were confined below, and thus effectually precluded them from
coming up. This abominable system is, I understand, pretty generally practised on board the slavers
from Bahia and Cuba.

In the Sierra Leone Advertiser of November 20,
1824, we have some striking instances of the frauds
practised by the Portuguese slavers in carrying on
their trade. Of three vessels captured, it appeared
that the Diana had a royal licence to carry 300
slaves, as being a vessel of 120 tons ; and this in
accordance with the law allowing five slaves to every
two tons (equal to three tons British) ; but in fact
she admeasured only sixty-six tons, which would give
a rate of five slaves to *one* ton. She had shipped at
Badagry, for Brazil, 156 slaves, besides her crew,
eighteen in number.

The Two Brazilian Friends, licensed to carry 365
slaves, as being of 146 tons, proved to be of only 95
tons ; and the platform for the men only two feet six
inches in height ; yet she had on board 260 slaves,
besides a crew of eighteen persons.

The Aviso, asserted to be 231, found to be only
165 tons ; 465 slaves were stowed in this vessel,
with a crew thirty-three in number.

A great many deaths had occurred in these vessels, and the survivors were in a very emaciated state.*

The Paris petition of — February, 1825, states, " That it is established, by authentic documents, that the slave captains throw into the sea, every year, about 3000 negroes, men, women, and children ; of whom more than half are thus sacrificed, whilst yet alive, either to escape from the visits of cruisers, or because, worn down by their sufferings, they could not be sold to advantage."†

In the Appendix (G) to the Report of the African Institution for 1827, we have the case of the schooner

---

* " ' Of all the vessels I was on board of,' says Captain Wool-combe, ' this (the Diana) was in the most deplorable condition; the stench from the accumulation of dirt, joined to that of so many human beings packed together in a small space (the men all ironed in pairs), was intolerable. To add to the scene of misery, the small-pox had broken out among them.'

" Commodore Bullen, who visited the Two Brazilian Friends, says, ' Its filthy and horrid state beggars all description. Many females were far advanced in pregnancy, and several had infants from four to twelve months of age; all were crowded together in one mass of living corruption; and yet this vessel had not her prescribed complement by nearly 100.'

" Commodore Bullen found the Aviso in a most crowded and wretched condition, although she had on board 120 less than directed in her passport. Such were the filth and crowd, that not one-half could have reached the Brazils alive. At the date of her capture she had scarcely 20 days' provisions for the slaves, and less water. ' How they intended to subsist them till their arrival at Bahia,' says the Captain, ' is to me a problem, unless they could have calculated on a great decrease from death.' " [1]

[1] Afr. Inst. Report for 1825, pp. 27, 28.

† Ib., 1826, pp. 62, 63.

L'Espoir, as narrated by General Milius, governor of Bourbon. " In the month of September, 1826, the schooner left the Mauritius under English colours, shaping its course towards the coasts of Madagascar. The Sieur Lemoine was the master; he fell in with a Portuguese vessel laden with negroes and gold-dust. An eagerness and thirst of gain seized upon his soul; he ran alongside of the Portuguese vessel, and immediately killed the mate by a musket-shot; having boarded her, he soon obtained possession of the vessel attacked, and his first questions were addressed to a Portuguese colonel, aged fifty, of whom he inquired where the money and gold-dust were deposited. After this short interrogatory, Lemoine purposely stepped aside, and a man named Reineur, who was behind him, with a pistol blew out the unfortunate colonel's brains. The master of the captured vessel, alarmed by the rapid succession of these massacres, threw himself overboard, in order to escape a more immediate death. Vain hope! the fury of Lemoine and his accomplices was not yet allayed. They pursued him in a boat, and, having soon overtaken him, they cut him on the head with a sabre. The unfortunate man, feeling himself wounded, caught hold, in order to support himself, of the boat in which his murderers were, who, profiting by this last effort of despair, had the dastard cruelty to run a sword into his throat, the point of which came out at his side: the body disappeared, and they returned on board, fatigued but not satiated with murder.

They shut up in the hold the remaining Portuguese
sailors, and, after taking off the rich cargo, they
scuttled the ship, and sunk her with the crew they
had thus shut up.

" This is one of many proofs of the piratical habits
and cruelty produced by the Slave Trade."*

In the evidence before the Committee on Sierra
Leone, &c., in 1830, we find it stated, by Lieutenant Tringham, that about 1825, the vessel in which
he sailed captured a slave-schooner of seventy or
eighty tons, bound for Brazil, with 280 slaves on
board.   There were about 100 on deck and 180
below.   They were so crowded on deck, that (as
the witness says) " We were not able to work the
vessel without treading on them."   As to their provisions, he remarked that the " jerked beef" was very
salt, and that there was always a scarcity of water :
" the allowance was about a pint a-day ; they had
two meals in the day, and about half a pint at each
meal was their full allowance."†

In the Despatches of Sir Charles MacCarthy,
dated the 3rd of August, 1822, I find the case of
the San José Hallaxa, a schooner under seven tons
burden, which was captured, by H.M.B. Thistle, in
the river Calabar ; and it appears, by the acknow-
ledgment of the master, that he shipped at Duke
Ephraim's Town, on that river, thirty slaves ; that
he had gone to sea with that number on board, in-

* Afr. Inst. Report, 1827.   App. G., p. 144.
† Parl. Report.   Sierra Leone, &c., 1830, p. 33.

tending to proceed to Princes Island, but, not having been able to make that port, he had returned to Calabar, having his provisions and water nearly expended, after having been at sea five or six weeks.

During this voyage, ten unfortunate objects of his avarice, not being able to procure sufficient nourishment to satisfy the cravings of nature, had been released from further sufferings by starvation! One poor female, in the absence of food, had existed on salt water until her faculties were destroyed, and she became raving mad; but even the deplorable and affecting state of insanity did not shield her from the brutal outrage of her oppressors, who, with a view of stifling her cries by frequent repetition of the lash, literally flogged her to death. The owner of this vessel, and the purchaser of these human beings, is a woman!—Donna Maria de Cruz, daughter of the notorious Gomez, formerly governor of Princes Island, and now holding the appointment of fiscal, and member of council. This woman is known to the Mixed Commission Court, having been under their cognizance some time since as proprietor of the " Conceição," condemned by the British and Portuguese judges."*

Sir John Barrow, in his able observations on the Slave Trade in 1826, says:—" We have also discovered among the papers before us (those laid before Parliament), that the amiable Donna Maria de Cruz, daughter of the governor of Princes Island, of

* Parl. Paper, 11th July, 1823, p. 9.

whom we had occasion once before to make honourable mention, is still engaged in carrying on the
traffic, though in a small way. The Victor sloop-
of-war fell in with and captured a schooner-boat belonging to this paragon of her sex, called the Maria
Pequina. Her burden was five tons. She had taken
on board in the river Gaboon, besides her crew, water,
and provisions, twenty-three slaves, six of whom had
already died; they were stowed in a space between
the water-casks and the deck, of eighteen inches in
height; and Lieutenant Scott reports that, when he
seized her, the remaining negroes were in a state of
actual starvation."*

Commodore Bullen, in his despatch of 26th November, 1826, describing the capture of *Le Daniel*,
says, " in consequence of the heavy rain which commenced shortly after I brought him to,—the slaves
quarrelled among themselves regarding the right of
precedence of those below to get on deck for fresh
air, and those who had already the possession of it,
when, shocking to relate, 19 fell victims."† The Commissioners at Havana, in their despatch of the 28th
August, 1828, mention the case of the " Intrepido,"
which, out of a cargo of 343, lost 190 in her passage,
and 18 after capture, making a total of 208. They
attribute a certain portion of this mortality to two in-
surrections of the negroes on board, but principally

* Edinburgh Review, No. 44, 1826.
† Class A, 1829, p. 138.

to the horrible confinement of so great a number on board so small a vessel.*

"The Invincible had on board a cargo of 440 negroes, a number, it seems, sixty-three short of her full complement; but these so crowded together that it became absolutely impossible to separate the sick from the healthy; and dysentery, ophthalmia, and scurvy breaking out among them, the provisions and water being of the worst kind, and the filth and stench beyond all description, 186 of the number had perished in less than sixty days."†

The Maria, 133 Spanish tons burden, captured by H.M.B. Plumper, 26th December, 1830, was found to contain 545 persons, including the crew,—thus allowing only the unprecedented small space of one ton for the accommodation of four persons; the consequence was, that though she was out only eleven days, the small-pox, dysentery, and other diseases had broken out with great virulence.‡

Captain Wauchope, R.N., late of the Thalia, has stated to me, that while on service with the preventive squadron in 1828, H.M.S. Medina, in which he sailed, captured the Spanish brig El Juan, with 407 slaves on board. It appeared that, owing to a press of sail during the chase, the El Juan had heeled so much, as to alarm the negroes, who made a rush to the grating. The crew thought they were attempt-

* Class A., 1829, p. 153.
† Afr. Inst. Report, 1827, pp. 4, 5.
‡ Class A. 1832, p. 13.

ing to rise, and getting out their arms, they fired upon
the wretched slaves through the grating, till all was
quiet in the hold.   When Captain Cassel went on
board, the negroes were brought up, one living and
one dead shackled together ; " it was an awful scene
of carnage and blood ; one mass of human gore :
Captain Cassel said he never saw anything so horrible in his life."

Dr. Walsh, in his "Notices of Brazil," gives a
most animated picture of the state of a Spanish slaver,
detained by the vessel of war, in which he returned
from Brazil, in May, 1829.   He says, "When we
mounted her decks we found her full of slaves ; she
had taken on board 562, and had been out seventeen
days, during which she lost fifty-five.   The slaves
were all enclosed under grated hatchways between
decks.   The space was so low that they sat between
each other's legs, and stowed so close together that
there was no possibility of their lying down, or at all
changing their position by night or day.   As they
belonged to, and were shipped on account of different
individuals, they were all branded like sheep, with
the owners' marks of different forms.   These were
impressed under their breasts, or on their arms ; and,
as the mate informed me with perfect indifference,
' burnt with the red-hot iron.' "

After many other particulars, the statement of
which my limits will not admit, Dr. Walsh continues : " The poor beings were all turned up together.   They came swarming up like bees from the

aperture of a hive, till the whole deck was crowded
to suffocation from stem to stern.   On looking into
the places where they had been crammed, there were
found some children next the sides of the ship.   The
little creatures seemed indifferent as to life or death,
and when they were carried on deck many of them
could not stand.   Some water was brought; it was
then that the extent of their sufferings was exposed
in a fearful manner.   They all rushed like maniacs
towards it.   No entreaties, or threats, or blows could
restrain them; they shrieked and struggled and fought
with one another for a drop of the precious liquid, as
if they grew rabid at the sight of it.   There is nothing
which slaves during the middle passage suffer from
so much, as want of water.   It is sometimes usual to
take out casks filled with sea-water as ballast, and
when the slaves are received on board, to start the
casks, and refill them with fresh.   On one occasion
a ship from Bahia neglected to change the contents
of the casks, and on the mid-passage, found to their
horror, that they were filled with nothing but salt-
water.   All the slaves on board perished!   We
could judge of the extent of their sufferings, from the
sight we now saw.   When the poor creatures were
ordered down again, several of them came and pressed
their heads against our knees with looks of the greatest anguish, at the prospect of returning to the horrid place of suffering below.   It was not surprising
that they had lost fifty-five, in the space of seventeen
days.   Indeed, many of the survivors were seen lying

about the decks in the last stage of emaciation, and in a state of filth and misery not to be looked at."

" While expressing my horror at what I saw, and exclaiming against the state of this vessel, I was informed by my friends, who had passed so long a time on the coast of Africa, and visited so many ships, that this was one of the best they had seen. The height sometimes between decks, was only eighteen inches; so that the unfortunate beings could not turn round, or even on their sides, the elevation being less than the breadth of their shoulders; and here they are usually chained to the decks by the neck and legs. After much deliberation, this wretched vessel was allowed to proceed on her voyage."

" It was dark when we separated; and the last parting sounds we heard from the unhallowed ship were the cries and shrieks of the slaves, suffering under some bodily infliction."*

In the same year, 1829, the Commissioners at Havana reported, that " The Fama de Cadiz came into port, having previously landed 300 slaves at Santa Cruz. It is said that this notorious slave-trader and pirate had plundered other slave-vessels on the coast of Africa of about 980 slaves, and had scarcely sailed for Cuba, when the small-pox and other contagious diseases broke out, which reduced the crew of 157 to 66, and her slaves to about 300; of whom the greatest part are in so wretched a

* Walsh's Notices of Brazil. London, 1830. Vol. ii. p. 475, &c.

state that her owners have been selling them as low as 100 dollars."

They also report the arrival of the schooner Constantia in ballast, after having landed seventy slaves on the coast. She is said to have left Africa with 438 negroes, who have been reduced by the small-pox to the above small number. And they add, " The mortality on board the slave-vessels this year has been truly shocking."*

In 1829 we have the case of the Midas. This vessel left the Bonny with a cargo of 560 slaves, and had only 400 on board at the time of detention. Of these, after the surrender, about thirty threw themselves into the sea. Before she arrived at Havana, nine other negroes had thrown themselves overboard, sixty-nine had died of the small-pox and other diseases. After their arrival ten more died. The remainder, 282, were then in a most dreadful state; so ill and so emaciated, that " It has hitherto been impossible," says the medical officer, " to make out the descriptions of their persons and marks that are inserted in their certificates of emancipation."†

In 1831 Captain Hamilton thus writes to the Commissioners :—" On our getting into Bahia, in the afternoon of the same day, I sent two officers on board the Destimida to search. They, after some time, and with much difficulty, discovered fifty male negro slaves concealed in the bottom of the vessel."‡

* Class A. 1829, p. 156.   † Class A. 1829, p. 148.
‡ Class A. 1831, p. 127.

" Five young men were extricated from one water-butt; but the greater part had been stowed or forced into the small or close spaces between the water-casks under the false decks."*

Captain Hayes, R.N., mentions the case of a slaver, having a large cargo of human beings, chained together : " The master of the vessel, with more humanity than his fellows, permitted some of them to come on deck (but still chained together) for the benefit of the air, when they immediately commenced jumping overboard, hand in hand, and drowning in couples." He explains the cause of this circumstance by saying, " they were just brought from a situation between decks, and to which they knew they must return, where the scalding perspiration was running from one to the other, covered also with their own filth, and where it is no uncommon occurrence for women to be bringing forth children, and men dying by their side, with, full in their view, living and dead bodies chained together, and the living, in addition to all their other torments, labouring under the most famishing thirst (being in very few instances allowed more than a pint of water a-day). He goes on to say, " I have now an officer on board the ' Dryad,' who, on examining one of these slave-vessels, found, not only living men chained to dead bodies, but the latter in a putrid state ; and we have now a case which, if true, is too horrible and disgusting to be described."†

* Class B. 1831, p. 117.   † Class B. 1831, p. 170.

In the same year (1831), the Black Joke and Fair Rosamond fell in with the Rapido and Regulo, two slave-vessels off the Bonny River. On perceiving the cruisers, they attempted to regain the port, and pitched overboard upwards of 500 human beings chained together before they were captured. From the abundance of sharks in the river their track was literally a blood-stained one."*

The master of an English merchant-vessel, who happened to be in the Bonny, at the time, witnessed the whole affair. He lately told me, that "The chase was so vigorous, and the slavers so anxious to escape, that the four vessels came flying into the creek, nearly all together, and ran aground in the mud, where the slavers threw overboard what remained of the negroes, very few of whom, from their being shackled together, reached the shore ; and that he and his crew helped to get the vessels again afloat, which was accomplished with much difficulty. He afterwards met the captain of one of the slavers, who justified what he had done as an act which necessity compelled him to adopt, for the preservation of his property."

Captain Ramsay, who at the time commanded the Black Joke, has stated to me, that during the chase he and his men distinctly saw the sharks tearing the bodies of the negroes who were thrown overboard by the slavers; and that had it not been for the fortunate rescue of two of the slaves of the

* Laird, vol. ii. p. 372.

K

Rapido, who had been flung into the sea shackled together, and who were brought up from under water by a boat-hook, that vessel would have escaped condemnation, as all her slaves had been thrown overboard or landed in canoes, before they came up with her.*

Captain Wauchope has informed me, that on the voyage out to Africa, about three years ago, his vessel captured a Portuguese slaver, and that when the prize-officer went on board, the Portuguese captain asked him, if no slaves had been on board, could he have been taken? The officer answered, " No." " Then," said the Portuguese, " if I had known it, I would have thrown every one overboard."

In a letter which I received from Captain Wauchope, of date 13th August, 1838, he says, " In February, 1836, I was informed by Commander Puget, that the Spanish slaver, Argus, three months before this date, was chased by the Charybdis, Lieutenant Mercer; that during the chase ninety-seven slaves had been thrown overboard, and that a Spanish captain he had captured, declared he would never hesitate to throw the slaves overboard, to prevent being taken."

Were it not that the evidence on these cases is unexceptionable, we could not believe that there did exist human beings capable of uttering such sentiments, or of performing such infamous deeds.

* See an account of this case in the United Service Journal for 1833, part i., p. 505, &c.

Captain Wauchope in the same letter informs me, that on the 18th September, 1836, the Thalia captured the Portuguese brig Felix, 590 slaves on board. " After capture," he says, " I went on board, and such a scene of horror it is not easy to describe ; the long-boat on the booms, and the deck aft, were crowded with little children, sickly, poor little unhappy things, some of them rather pretty, and some much marked and tattoed ; much pains must have been taken by their miserable parents to ornament and beautify them.

" The women lay betwen decks aft, much crowded, and perfectly naked ; they were not barred down, the hatchway, a small one, being off ; but the place for the men was too horrible, the wretches, chained two and two, gasping and striving to get at the bars of the hatchways, and such a steam and stench as to make it intolerable even to look down. It requires much caution at first, in allowing them to go on deck, as it is a common practice for them to jump overboard to get quit of their misery.

" The slave-deck was not more than three feet six in height, and the human beings stowed, or rather crushed as close as possible ; many appeared very sickly. There was no way of getting into the slave-room but by the hatchway. I was told, when they were all on deck to be counted, that it was impossible for any of our people to go into the slave-room for a single minute, so intolerable was the stench The colour of these poor creatures was of a dark squalid yellow, so different from the fine glossy black of our liberated Africans and Kroomen. I was shown a man much bit and bruised; it was done in a struggle at the gratings of their hatchways for a mouthful of fresh air."

It is fearful to contemplate the increase, of late years, in the mortality during the middle passage. The chief reason, as it appears, is well given by Laird in his journal of the recent expedition to the Niger. He says :—" Instead of the large and commodious vessels which it would be the interest of the slave-trader to employ, we have by our interference, forced him to use a class of vessels, (well known to naval men as *American Clippers*,) of the very worst description that could have been imagined, for the purpose, every quality being sacrificed for speed. In the holds of these vessels the unhappy victims of European cupidity are stowed literally in bulk."[*]

It ought also to be kept in view, that there is this material difference betwixt these " clippers " and other merchant-vessels: that while the latter usually carry far more than their registered tonnage would seem to permit, the former invariably exhibit a capacity for a cargo greatly below the tonnage by registration.

As a proof of the increase in the mortality on the middle passage, I may adduce the evidence of Mr. Jackson (who had been a judge in the Mixed

---

[*] Laird, vol. ii. p. 369.

Commission Court at Sierra Leone) before the Committee on Sierra Leone, &c., in 1830. In answer to a question, he said, " I think the sufferings of those poor slaves are greatly aggravated by the course now adopted ; for the trade is now illegal ; and therefore whatever is done, is done clandestinely ; they are packed more like bales of goods on board than human beings, and the general calculation is, that if in three adventures one succeeds, the owners are well paid."*

Were it not that I feel bound to substantiate my case up to the present time, I would gladly pass over the numberless instances of cruelty and mortality connected with this branch of the subject, which are made known to us by the papers laid before Parliament within the last few years. But I shall notice some of these instances, as briefly as can be done, without suppressing the main facts which are established by them.

The Carolina, captured in 1834, off Wydah.† " This vessel was only seventy-five tons burden, yet she had 350 negroes crammed on board of her, 180 of whom were literally so stowed as to have barely sufficient height to hold themselves up, when in a sitting posture. The poor creatures crowded round their deliverers, with their mouths open and their tongues parched for want of water, presenting a perfect spectacle of human misery."

* Sierra Leone Report, 1830, p. 55.
† Class A. 1834, p. 17.

The Patacho, reported by the Commissioners at Rio de Janeiro in 1835. This " vessel was in the first instance detained only on suspicion, and the capturing party had had possession forty-eight hours, and had made every possible search, as they supposed, before it was discovered that there were any slaves concealed on board. What the state of these wretched beings, to the number of forty-seven, must have been, deprived for so long a time of air and food, and packed in the smallest possible compass, like so many bales of goods, we need not pain your Lordship by describing."*

In a letter from the the Cape of Good Hope, of date 20th January, 1837, we find it stated that Her Majesty's brig Dolphin had lately captured the corvette Incomprehensible ; and that, on taking possession of her, " the scene presented on board was harrowing in the extreme. One hundred had died from sickness, out of the 800 embarked ; another 100 were lying nearly lifeless on her decks, in wretchedness and misery, and all the agony of despair ; the remaining 600 were so cramped from the close manner in which they were packed (like herrings in a barrel), and the length of time they had been on their voyage, and the cold they had endured in rounding the Cape, in a state of nudity, that it took the utmost exertions of the English sailors, favoured by a hot sun, to straighten them." †

* Class A. 1835, p. 286.
† From a correspondent of the Times newspaper.

In the Shipping and Mercantile Gazette of 2nd June, 1838, is the following paragraph : " A letter from the ' Snake ' sloop of war, dated 31st March, 1838, says, ' We have captured a very fine schooner, called the Arogan, off Cape Antonio, having 350 slaves of both sexes, under the age of twenty, and have sent her into the Havana for adjudication. She cleared out from Gallinas, and lost fifty on her passage by death, owing to the crowded manner in which they were packed, resembling goods in a draper's shop.' "

In the parliamentary papers printed last year by the House of Commons, I observe the following cases reported :—" The brig Don Manuel de Portugal, from Angola, embarked 600 slaves ; of these seventy-three died on the voyage."

" Brig Adamastor, from Quilimane, embarked 800 slaves ; of these 304 died on the voyage !"

" Brig Leao, from Quilimane, embarked 855 slaves ; of these 283 died, or were thrown overboard alive, during the voyage. The small-pox having appeared among the slaves, thirty of them were immediately thrown overboard alive ; afterwards the measles made its appearance, of which 253 died. The remaining slaves, 572 in number, were landed on the coast of Brazil at Mozambayo, near to Ilha Grande, but in so miserable a state that the greater part could not walk, but were carried on shore."*

* Class B. 1837, p. 58.

" The brig Flor de Quilimane, from Quilimane, embarked 850 slaves; of these 163 died on the passage, and 697 were landed at Campos in a very sickly state."*

In a letter from a member of the Society of Friends, dated Havana, July 14th, 1836, and published in the Colonization Herald, Philadelphia, Aug. 15th, 1838, I find the following passage: " In company with an English naval officer, I made a visit across the bay to several of these slave-vessels. We were permitted to walk over them, but no particular attention was paid to us; on the contrary, we were looked upon with suspicion, and received short and unsatisfactory answers to our questions in general; all attempts to enter into conversation with those on board appeared useless. With one, however, we were more successful: an old weather-beaten Spaniard was walking the deck; although an old pirate, his expression of countenance was fine : taking a seat under the awning on the quarter-deck, offering him a bundle of cigaritas, and lighting one ourselves, by degrees induced him to enter into conversation, and, in the course of one hour or more, I learned from him some horrid truths. He told us that, in four voyages, he had brought in the vessel in which we were 1600 human beings; his was a fortunate vessel, and seldom lost more than half a dozen a-voyage; once, however, he told us, he was not so lucky; a malignant disease broke out on

* Class B. 1837, p. 60.

board soon after leaving the coast, and, of 300 taken in in Africa, but ninety-five were landed, more dead than alive, on the island.

"The materiel, such as handcuffs, chains, and even the lower-decks, are taken out and are fitted up on the coast of Africa. We saw the apertures in the decks to admit the air, and, as we were leaving the brig in our boat alongside, the captain exultingly told us that he knew we were officers of the British sloop of war, pointing to the Champion, which was riding at anchor at a little distance from us; 'but,' added he, 'you are welcome. I yesterday showed your captain (meaning of the Champion) all over my trim vessel. I have nothing to conceal—you dare not touch me here; and, once outside (with an expressive shrug of the shoulders), you may catch me if you can.'"

We have little authentic information as to the transport of the slaves from one part of the coast to another in south-east Africa, or from that coast to Arabia, and the other countries northwards, to which they are conveyed. But Captain Moresby, to whom I have already alluded, described to me the passage coastways, in the following terms:—"The Arab dows, or vessels, are large, unwieldy, open boats, without a deck. In these vessels temporary platforms of bamboos are erected, leaving a narrow passage in the centre. The negroes are then stowed, in the literal sense of the word, in bulk; the first along the floor of the vessel, two adults, side by side, with a boy or girl resting between or on them, until the tier is complete. Over them the first platform is laid, supported an inch or two clear of their bodies, when a second tier is stowed, and so on until they reach the gunwale of the vessel."

"The voyage, they expect, will not exceed twenty-four or forty-eight hours; it often happens that a calm, or unexpected land-breeze, delays their progress: in this case a few hours are sufficient to decide the fate of the cargo; those of the lower portion of the cargo that die cannot be removed. They remain until the upper part are dead, and thrown over, and, from a cargo of from 200 to 400 stowed in this way, it has been known that not a dozen, at the expiration of ten days, have reached Zanzebar. On the arrival of the vessels at Zanzebar, the cargo are landed; those that can walk up the beach are arranged for the inspection of the Imaum's officer, and the payment of duties—those that are weak or maimed by the voyage are left for the coming tide to relieve their miseries. An examination then takes place, which for brutality has never been exceeded in Smithfield."

In immediate connexion with the mortality incident to the middle passage I come now to the subject of

WRECKS, ETC.

In Appendix D. of the African Institution Report for 1820 we are told that a "Spanish brig, on arrival at Point à Petre, experienced a severe squall, and, on the captain opening the hatches (which were let down during the squall), he found fifty of the poor Africans dead."

In Appendix B. of the same report we find, in a statement of Sir G. Collier, Dec. 27, 1821, that the schooner Carlotta embarked, off Cape Palmas, "260 slaves; and the very next day, in a tornado off St. Ann's, for want of timely precaution, upset, and, dreadful to relate, the whole of these wretched people, confined in irons, sank with her."

In the parliamentary papers for 1822 we find, "The schooner Yeanam was separated from the other vessels in a dreadful storm, as they were proceeding to Havana, and sank, with 380 slaves on board."[*]

The Accession, an English brig, brought into Bahia thirty-nine negroes, whom she rescued from a wreck abandoned by its crew. Thirty-one were found holding by the top of a mast. On cutting the side of the vessel open, they took out ten more from an almost pestilential atmosphere, and saw a number lying dead. The crew, and 138 of the slaves, had been previously taken out by the Viajante; but, as that vessel was herself carrying 622 negroes, she had left these others to perish in the waves.[†]

I find, by an extract from the Sierra Leone Gazette of the 12th June, 1824, that, " on the appearance of H.M.S. Victor, a boat full of men was seen to leave

[*] Parl. Papers, 11th July, 1823, p. 7.
[†] Afr. Inst. Report, 1826, pp. 37, 38.

the lugger (l'Henrietta Aime), after which she got under weigh, but, instead of attempting to escape, run on shore in a heavy surf, where she immediately went to pieces; and, from the number of blacks observed on her decks, there can be no doubt she had her cargo of slaves on board, all of whom perished."

By the despatch of the Commissioners at Havana, of 26th February, 1826, it appears that "the Magico was fallen in with and chased by H.M.S. Union, and, having been brought to action in the course of the 21st January, she was finally run on shore on the morning of the 22nd, and shortly after taken possession of. The crew had previously escaped to land with (it is supposed) about 200 negroes; many, however, were left behind, severely wounded, some were hanging on at different parts of the vessel, and from twenty to thirty of their dead bodies were seen in the sea, evidently the consequence of the endeavours made to force them to jump overboard and swim to the shore. The crew even carried their barbarity so far as to leave a lighted match in the powdermagazine.*

In the parliamentary papers of 1827 I find the case of the "Teresa," a Spanish schooner, which was suddenly laid on her beam-ends by a tornado, and almost immediately went down, with 186 slaves on board.†

We have also the account of a wreck of a Portuguese slave-schooner, the Piombeter, at the Bahamas,

* Class A. 1827, p. 99.　　　　† Class A., 1827, p. 30.

on the 20th of January, 1837, communicated to me by Major M'Gregor, a special justice. He states that the vessel was under fifty tons burden, and that 180 slaves had been embarked in her; "they were chiefly fine young lads under fifteen years of age." About twenty had died before the wreck took place.

In another letter, dated Nov. 1, 1837, he states that several wrecks of slavers had taken place in his vicinity. As to one of these he says, " Last Friday, the 27th ult., a schooner vessel, under the Portuguese flag, was totally wrecked on the shore of Harbour Island, where I now reside in my official capacity, having upwards of 200 African slaves on board at the time, only fifty-three of which were saved ; the greater part of the ablest men, being chained together below at the time, were consequently drowned in the hold of the vessel. Sixty bodies have since been washed ashore, which I got interred ; upwards of twenty were drifted yesterday to the mouth of the harbour, who seem to have been fettered upon the deck, and grouped together in one heap. It is supposed that from fifty to sixty bodies are still remaining in the hold of the hull, now almost imbedded in the sand. Attempts have been made to dive for the bodies, but without success, they being found so fast chained and crowded together, it was found impossible to remove them.

" I shall not shock your feelings by entering into the details of the abominable conduct of the captain and crew of this vessel during the passage towards some of the most youthful and best-looking on board; this was brought to my knowledge by two of the Africans, who speak Portuguese, and one who speaks a little broken English. They appear to have conducted themselves more like demons than human beings.

"This slaver, named the Invincible, took in the Africans at Port Prague, Cape de Verd Islands, and was bound for Matanzas in the island of Cuba."

In a letter from Colonel Nicolls, at the Bahamas, of date 1st August, 1837,* it is stated that " the Esperanza, a Spanish slave-schooner, had been wrecked on one of these islands during the preceding month. It was ascertained that this vessel had embarked 320 negroes on the coast of Africa; of these only 220 were landed at the time of the wreck. It appears that between sixty and seventy murders had been committed during the voyage on the helpless Africans; and in this manner:—When any of the slaves refused their food or became sick, the boatswain's mate, with a weighty club, struck them on the back of the neck, when they fell, and were thrown overboard."

I make the following extract from the Jamaica Watchman, of 29th May, 1838:—"A report having reached Port Royal, that a Spanish schooner, having on board upwards of 300 Africans, had been stranded off the Pedro shoals, H. M. ship Nimrod,

* Communicated to me by his brother, Col. Nicolls, R.M.

and the Hornet schooner, sailed yesterday morning for the purpose of taking her cargo, and bringing them into port." "The vessels of war humanely sent to seek the unfortunate Africans on board the slaver lately wrecked on the Pedro reefs, have returned, bringing the melancholy information that no traces of them could be found.   The vessel had gone to pieces, and 300 human beings consigned to a watery grave. The crew had taken to their boats and landed at Black River." *

Captain Wilson, R.N., in a letter on this subject, dated 9th January, 1839, says; "I have overhauled many slave-ships, and freely confess that it is impossible to exaggerate the horrors they exhibit ; they are all very much alike, the greater or less misery depending, usually, upon the size of the vessel, and the time they might have been embarked, as every day brings with it a fearful increase of disease, desperation, imbecility, and death."

Passing over hundreds of cases of a description similar to those which I have noticed, I have now done with these heart-sickening details; and the melancholy truth is forced upon us, that, notwith-

---

* I lately learnt, that the " Aguila Vengadora," had arrived at Havana, under the name of the " Esplorador," on the 30th June, 1838, with 200 negroes, the remnant of a cargo of 560. During her passage from Mozambique, she encountered a storm, which compelled the crew to close the hatches on the negroes for two days. When the storm abated, it appeared that about 300 had perished from hunger and suffocation.

standing all that has been accomplished, the cruelties and horrors of the passage across the Atlantic have increased; nay, more, they have been aggravated by the very efforts which we have made for the abolition of the traffic.

" Facts too, like these just mentioned, are not extraordinary incidents, selected and remembered as such. They are hourly occurrences of the trade; and as they are found in every instance where detection affords an opportunity of inquiry, it is absurd to suppose that the undetected slave-vessel is exempted from scenes of similar cruelty. It may fairly be assumed, that greater cruelty does not obtain in the one vessel which is captured, than in the one hundred which escape. Some of these have made eleven, some thirteen, successful voyages, and there is little doubt that similar acts of atrocity have been perpetrated in all—that all have been marked by the same accumulation of human agony, and the same waste of human life."*

I will endeavour to give a

SUMMARY

of the extent of the mortality incident to the middle passage. Newton states, that in his time, it amounted to one-fourth, on the average, of the number embarked.†

From papers presented to the House of Lords, in 1799, it appears that, in the year 1791, (three years

---

* Afr. Inst. Report for 1825, p. 31.   † Newton, p. 36.

after the passing of the Slave Carrying Regulation Act,) of 15,754 negroes embarked for the West Indies, &c., 1378 died during the passage, the average length of which was fifty-one days, showing a mortality of 8¾ per cent.

The amount of the mortality in 1792 was still greater. Of 31,554 slaves carried from Africa, no fewer than 5413 died on the passage, making somewhat less than 17 per cent., in fifty-one days.*

Captain Owen, in a communication to the Admiralty, on the Slave Trade with the eastern coast of Africa, in 1823, states—" That the ships which use this traffic, consider they make an excellent voyage if they save one-third of the number embarked ;" " some vessels are so fortunate as to save one-half of their cargo alive."†

Captain Cook says, in the communication to which I have before alluded, as to the East coast traffic, " If they meet with bad weather, in rounding the Cape, their sufferings are beyond description ; and in some instances, one-half of the lives on board are sacrificed. In the case of the ' Napoleon,' from Quilimane, the loss amounted to two-thirds. It was stated to me by Captains and Supercargos of other slavers, that they made a profitable voyage if they lost fifty per cent ; and that this was not uncommon."

Caldcleugh says, " scarcely two-thirds live to be landed."‡

* Debates in Parliament, 1806, Ap. p. 191.
† Class B. 1825, p. 41.   ‡ Vol. i. p. 56.

L

Governor M'Lean, of Cape Coast, who has had many opportunities of acquiring information on the subject, has stated to me, that he considers the average of deaths on the passage, to amount to one-third.

Captain Ramsay, R.N., who was a long time on service with the Preventive Squadron, also stated to me, that the mortality on the passage across the Atlantic must be greater than the loss on the passage to Sierra Leone, from the greater liberty allowed after capture, and from the removal of the shackles. He believes the average loss to be one-third.

Rear Admiral Sir Graham Eden Hamond, Commander-in-Chief on the South American station, in 1834, thus writes to the British Consul at Monte Video :—" A slave-brig of 202 tons was brought into this port with 521 slaves on board. The vessel is said to have cleared from Monte Video in August last, under a licence to import 650 African colonists.

" The licence to proceed to the Coast of Africa is accompanied by a curious document, purporting to be an application from two Spaniards at Monte Video, named Villaca and Barquez, for permission to import 650 colonists, and 250 *more—to cover the deaths on the voyage.*"*

Here we have nearly one-third given, apparently for the average loss on the passage, and this, estimated by the slave-dealers themselves on the American side of the Atlantic.

I come next to consider the loss after capture.

* Class B. 1835, p. 141.

LOSS AFTER CAPTURE.

It is melancholy to reflect, that the efforts which we have so long and so perseveringly made for the abolition of the Slave Trade, should not only have been attended with complete failure, but with an increase of negro mortality. A striking example of the truth of this remark is afforded, when we consider the great loss of negro life which annually takes place subsequently to the capture of the slave-vessels, on their passage to South America and the West Indies.

I do not intend, in this part of my subject, to discuss the merits of the construction of the Mixed Commission Courts, or their forms of proceeding; nor do I propose, here, to say anything as to the preference which it appears to me, ought to be given to Fernando Po, over Sierra Leone, as a station for a Commission Court, and a depôt for liberated Africans; my purpose for the present is, merely to state the facts which have come to my knowledge, with the requisite evidence, bearing on the mortality after capture.

Admiral Hamond, in a despatch to the Admiralty on this subject, in the year 1834, puts the case of a

slaver overloaded with negroes, many of them in a
sickly or dying state, captured and brought into Rio
Janeiro, (as in the case of the ' Rio de la Plata,')
where the miserable slaves confined to the vessel, in
a hot and close port, must await the tardy process of
the Mixed Commission Court : and he goes on to say,
that in such a case, " the stopping of the slave-vessel
is only exposing the blacks to greater misery, and a
much greater chance of speedy death, than if they
were left to their original destination of slavery."*

In the 21st Report of the African Institution, we
have the case of the Pauleta, captured off Cape Formosa, in February, 1826, by " Lieutenant Tucker,
H. M. Ship Maidstone, with 221 slaves on board.
Her burden was only 69 tons, and into this space
were thrust 82 men, 56 women, 39 boys, and 44
girls. The only provision found on board for their
subsistence, was yams of the worst quality, and fetid
water. When captured, both small-pox and dysentery had commenced their ravages ; 30 died on the
passage to Sierra Leone, and the remainder were
landed in an extreme state of wretchedness and emaciation."†

In 1830, a Committee of the House of Commons
was appointed to consider the relative merits of Sierra
Leone and Fernando Po. Captain Bullen stated in
evidence before the Committee, that the Aviso, captured near Fernando Po, took five weeks to reach
Sierra Leone, during which time forty-five of the

* Class B. 1835, p. 66.   † Afr. Inst. Report for 1827, p. 9.

slaves died : and that in the case of the Segunda Rosalia, the passage occupied eleven weeks, during which more than 120 of the slaves were lost.[*]

Lieutenant Tringham informed the Committee that he carried a Spanish schooner up to Sierra Leone as prize-master. She had 480 slaves on board at the time of capture. The voyage to Sierra Leone occupied six weeks, and 110 slaves died on the passage. In answer to the question " If you had had to have taken the vessel to Fernando Po for adjudication, instead of Sierra Leone, the lives of those persons would have been saved ?" he replied, " I think so." He afterwards said, that the average voyage of the vessels he had taken from the Bights of Benin and Biafra to Sierra Leone, was five weeks.[†]

Mr. Jackson stated to the Committee, that the condition of the slaves, at the time of capture, was " most deplorable, as to disease, and as to the mortality which has ensued : in one instance, 179 out of 448 slaves, on board of one vessel, died in their passage up ; in another, 115 out of 271. In all, with only one exception, the numbers have been considerable."[‡]

Mr. John McCormack, in his evidence, said, that on going aboard slave-vessels after capture and the passage to Sierra Leone, he generally found the slaves who had been any length of time on the voyage, " in a most miserable state of debility." And he

* Sierra Leone Report, 1830, p. 8.   † Ib., p. 32.
‡ Ib., p. 52.

adds, "They unavoidably must, from the description of the vessels, suffer very greatly; many of these vessels have not more than three feet between decks, and no air can get to them except what comes down the hatchways. They are so low in the water, no airports can be cut in their sides."*

In the Appendix to the Report of this Committee, a return is given for the period between 10th August, 1819, and 11th October, 1829,

Of slaves captured	25,212
Landed at Sierra Leone, or Fernando Po	21,563
Loss on the passage	3,649†

Being nearly one-seventh, or about 14 per cent: and this almost entirely on the passage to Sierra Leone.

Mr. Rankin, in his Visit to Sierra Leone, tells us of a Portuguese schooner, the Donna Maria da Gloria, which he saw there, with a cargo of slaves on board. She had embarked them at Loando, in August, 1833, and was captured by H. M. B. Snake. The captor took the vessel to Rio; but the Brazilian Mixed Commission Court would not entertain the case; he was therefore obliged to send her to Sierra Leone, where she arrived on February 4, 1834. On her arrival, it was ascertained that she had lost 95 out of 430 slaves. A long process ensued before the Mixed Commission Court, the result of which was the liberation of the vessel; and at this

* Sierra Leone Report, p. 66.   † Ib., Ap. p. 122.

period, her state is thus described : " Notwithstanding the exertions of Mr. Thomas Frazer, assistant-surgeon of the capturing ship, who continued to administer to them while himself in a state of extreme suffering and danger, before reaching Sierra Leone, 104 had died, and 64 more (in a state that moved the heart even of the slave-crew) were voluntarily landed by the master, and taken charge of by the liberated African department. The miserable remnant, in a state impossible to describe, afflicted with ophthalmia, dysentery, and frightful ulcers, and showing, also, some symptoms of small-pox, left the harbour of Sierra Leone ; the slaves having been then on board 165 days, 137 having elapsed since her capture : and of her original cargo of 430,240 alone remained."*

Dr. Cullen, of Edinburgh, who lately returned from Rio de Janeiro, after a five years' residence there, thus writes to Lord Glenelg, of date 28th February, 1838, in reference to the Donna Maria having been released at Sierra Leone : " Some months after this, they were met by a Brazilian ship of war, near Bahia, in distress ; and their numbers reduced to 170."†

Mr. Rankin visited La Pantica, another vessel which had been brought into Sierra Leone. " The ship," he says, " was thronged with men, women, and children, all entirely naked, and

---

* Rankin's Visit, &c., vol. ii. p. 96.
† Class A (Further Series), 1837, p. 91.

disgusting with disease : 274 were at this moment in the little schooner. When captured, 315
had been found on board, forty had died during the
voyage from Old Calebar. Of the remainder, 8 or
10 died in the first week after liberation. The majority of the survivors were miserably persecuted by
ophthalmia and dysentery, and 50 were sent to the
hospital, for fever, at Kissey."*

In a report of the Sierra Leone Commissioners,
dated 4th February, 1835,† it is stated that " the
Sutil arrived in this harbour on the 23rd ult., with 228
slaves on board, 79 having died on the passage to
this port, whilst the vessel was in charge of the captors, in addition to a frightful loss of life which had
previously occurred on the first night of the voyage,
owing to a ferocious scramble for room, amongst the
densely-crowded negroes, and by which many were
suffocated and killed. The surgeon to the courts
immediately visited the slaves, and reported that there
were 21 men and boys, and 8 girls, sick with dysentery, many of them being in an advanced stage of the
disease."

In the Falmouth Packet of the 8th of December
last, I find the following statement : " The Brilliant,
captured by H.M.S. Rover, on the 11th April, 1838,
had 289 negroes on board ; but, owing to the delays
which kept them in their horrible state of imprisonment on board, were daily dying, and from that time

* Rankin, vol. ii. p. 1   † Class A. 1835, p. 48.

to the 16th of September, 119 of these miserable
creatures had died. When the Buffalo left, the small-
pox and dysentery had broken out, and was sweeping
them at the rate of 8 and 10 per day."

The following list of seventeen vessels, most of
which were captured in the Bights of Benin and
Biafra, and brought for adjudication to Sierra Leone,
will serve to exhibit the loss after capture in a forcible
manner :—

Where con-demned.	Vessel's Name.	Nation.	Number on board.	Died before Adjudi-cation.	Refer-ence. Class A	Page.
Havana. Sierra Leone.	Emelia	Spanish	282	107	1828	39
	Invincival	Portuguese	440	190	,,	59
	Clementina	Brazilian	471	115	1829	82
	Ceres	do.	279	151	1830	64
	Arcinia	do.	448	179	,,	38
	Mensageira	do.	353	109	,,	58
	Midas	Spanish	562	281	,,	148
	Constancia*	do.	438	368*	,,	162
	Fama da Cadiz†	do.	980	680†	,,	156
Havana. Sierra Leone.	Christina	do.	348	132	1831	21
	Tentadora	Brazilian	432	112	,,	54
	Umbellina	do.	377	214	,,	65
	Formidable	Spanish	712	304	1835	50
	Sutil	do.	335	124	,,	48
	Minerva	do.	725	208	,,	56
	Marte	do.	600	197	,,	163
	Diligencia	do.	210	90	,,	200
			7992	3561		

* This vessel was not brought before the Court.   The numbers are
given on the authority of Mr. Commissary Judge Macleay.
    † The same of the Fama da Cadiz.

Showing a loss on these selected cases of 44 per
cent. !

In 1830, the Committee of the House of Commons came to the following resolution : that captured vessels are, " on an average, upwards of five weeks on their passage from the place of capture to Sierra Leone, occasioning a loss of the captured slaves amounting to from *one-sixth to one-half* of the whole number, while the survivors are generally landed in a miserable state of weakness and debility."*

I have not adverted to Rio de Janeiro, or the Havana, on this head, because there are very few captures on the American side of the Atlantic, and when captures do occur, the time consumed in the passage to either of these ports is little, if at all, more than what would have been required for completing the voyage.

But it appears to be demonstrated, by evidence which cannot be impugned, that the loss *after capture* on the African side of the Atlantic, varies from *one-sixth to one-half of the whole number*.

LOSS AFTER LANDING AND IN THE SEASONING.

The last head of mortality, is that which occurs after landing from the slave vessel, and in the seasoning.

We are here again obliged to go back, for information, to the evidence at the end of the last century ; but in this branch of the subject, so far as can be ascertained, there has been no improvement ; on the contrary, the slaves are now subjected to greater

* Sierra Leone Report, 1830, p. 4.

hardships, in their being landed and concealed as smuggled goods, than they were in former times, when a slave-vessel entered the ports of Rio Janeiro and Havana as a fair trader, and openly disposed of her cargo.

Mr. Falconbridge, whose evidence has already been largely quoted, tells us, that on being landed the negroes are sold, sometimes by what is termed a *scramble;* " but previous thereto," he adds, " the sick or refuse slaves, of which there are frequently many, are usually conveyed on shore, and sold at a tavern by public auction. These, in general, are purchased by the Jews and surgeons, but chiefly upon speculation, at so low a price as five or six dollars a-head.

" I was informed," he says, " by a Mulatto woman, that she purchased a sick slave at Grenada upon speculation, for the small sum of one dollar, as the poor wretch was apparently dying of the flux. It seldom happens that any who are carried ashore in the emaciated state to which they are generally reduced by that disorder, long survive their landing. I once saw sixteen conveyed on shore, and sold in the foregoing manner, the whole of whom died before I left the island, which was within a short time after." Various are the deceptions made use of in the disposal of the sick slaves, and many of these such as must excite in every humane mind the liveliest sensations of horror. I have been well informed that a Liverpool captain boasted of his having cheated some Jews by the following stratagem : " A lot of slaves afflicted

with the flux, being about to be landed for sale, he
directed the surgeon to . . . .
. . . . . Thus prepared, they were landed and
taken to the accustomed place of sale, where, being
unable to stand, unless for a very short time, they are
usually permitted to sit.   The Jews, when they examine them, oblige them to stand up . . . . .
. . . . and when they do not perceive
this appearance, they consider it as a symptom of
recovery.   In the present instance, such an appearance being prevented, the bargain was struck, and
they were accordingly sold.   But it was not long
before a discovery ensued.   The excruciating pain,
which the prevention occasioned, not being to be borne
by the poor wretches, was removed, and the deluded
purchasers were speedily convinced of the imposi-
tion."*

In the report of the African Institution for
1818, the case of the Joachim, a Portuguese slave-
vessel, is noticed; and Lieutenant Eicke, after stating
the wretched condition of the slaves at and subsequent
to the time of capture, says, " That between the nine-
teenth and twenty-fourth day of their being landed,
thirteen more died, notwithstanding good provisions,
medical aid, and kind treatment, and *thirty more*
died between the 24th of February and 16th instant;
all occasioned, as he in his conscience is firmly persuaded, by the cruel and inhuman treatment of the
Portuguese owners; that more than 100 of them

* Falconbridge, p.33.

were at the time of their landing just like skeletons covered with skin, and moving by slow machinery, hardly maintaining the appearance of animated human beings. That the remainder of them were all enervated, and in a sickly state."*

In an official medical report as to the health of the liberated Africans at the Gambia, of date 31st of December, 1833, and drawn up by Mr. Foulis, Assistant-Surgeon of the Royal African Corps, and Dr. James Donovan, Acting Colonial Surgeon, it is stated, that the greater part of those, who are weak and emaciated on arrival, soon afterwards die; many, after a longer or shorter residence, fall into the same state, linger, and also perish from causes not very dissimilar. For this mortality, the medical board assigned, as probable causes, the long confinement in slave-houses previous to embarkation, want of cleanliness and ventilation while on board the slave-ships, alterations in dress, food, and habits, and, not the least, change of climate. These act directly, simultaneously, and banefully, on the system in a very great number of instances. But when the sad recollection of perpetual expatriation; the lacerated feelings of kindred and friendship; the rude violation of all the sacred and social endearments of country and relationship; the degrading anticipation of endless unmitigated bondage, are added to those, they act still more injuriously on the consti-

* Afr. Inst. Report, 1818, p. 28.

tution, although exerted through the medium of mind. The moral and physical combination of such extraordinary circumstances, concentrated with such fearful intensity, conjunctly creates disease in such a redoubtable shape, as to induce a belief that nothing similar has yet appeared in the annals of physic."*

Mr. Rankin, in his work on Sierra Leone, says,† "To the King's Yards I paid frequent visits, and found an interest awakened on behalf of the people. Of the women, many were despatched to the hospital at Kissey, victims to raging fevers. Others had become insane. I was informed that insanity is the frequent fate of the women captives, and that it chiefly comes upon such as at first exhibit most intellectual development, and greatest liveliness of disposition. Instances were pointed out to me. The women sustain their bodily sufferings with more silent fortitude than the men, and seldom destroy themselves; but they brood more over their misfortunes, until the sense of them is lost in madness."‡

Dr. Cullen,§ in his letter to Lord Glenelg, men-

---

* Records of the Colonial Office for 1833.

† Vol. ii. p. 124.   ‡ Ibid.

§ Dr. Cullen also writes, that, about the same time, a British cruiser, the Raleigh, Captain Quin, brought in a slaver, the Rio da Plata, with about 400 Africans on board, who were landed, and a guard placed over them; and that, "a few nights after they were put ashore, the guard was surprised in the middle of the night, by a band of fellows pretending to be justices of the

tions the following case : " About the beginning of
1834, a small schooner (I think the name was the
Duqueza de Braganza) was captured by one of Her
British Majesty's cruisers, and brought into Rio de
Janeiro, having on board between 300 and 400 Africans, mostly children ; these poor creatures had suffered much from their long confinement in such a
small vessel, and it is believed a great many had died
on the passage. By the humanity of the late Admiral
Sir Michael Seymour, they were taken on shore,
and properly cared for, otherwise the mortality
amongst them after landing must have been greater
than it was." He then says, that they were adjudged to be free.   At the time of the sentence of
the Court, " they were reduced by deaths to 288,
all of whom were sent to the house of correction, to
work for the Brazilian government.   I called at this
house of correction eight days after their arrival
there, when seven more had died, and there were
then thirty-five sick, confined in a small room, lying
on the floor, without bed or covering of any kind,
with their heads to the wall and their feet towards
the centre, leaving a narrow passage between the
rows.   The same day, I saw about 100 of these
children in an apartment on the ground-floor,
sitting all round on their heels, after the fashion

peace, who carried off 200 of the negroes, and next day no traces
of them could be found.   Those that remained were taken to the
house of correction, and disposed of in the Brazilian fashion[1]. "

[1] Class A (Farther Series), 1837, p. 91.

of the country, and looking most miserable. On the November following, I again visited the house of correction, and learned that out of the 288, sent there in June, 107 had died, and a great many more were sick."*

In the letter from Havana, dated in 1838, from which I have already quoted, the following account is given: " In the cool of the evening we made a visit to the bazaar. A newly imported cargo of 220 human beings were here exposed for sale. They were crouched down upon their forms around a large room : during a visit of more than an hour that we were there, not a word was uttered by one of them. On entering the room, the eyes of all were turned towards us, as if to read in our countenances their fate ; they were all nearly naked, being but slightly clad in a light check shirt, upon which was a mark upon the breast ; with a few exceptions they were but skin and bone, too weak to support their languid forms ; they were reclining on the floor, their backs resting against the wall. When a purchaser came they were motioned to stand, which they obeyed, though with apparent pain ; a few were old and grey; but the greater proportion were mere children, of from ten to thirteen or fifteen years of age ; when they stood, their legs looked as thin as reeds, and hardly capable of supporting the skeletons of their wasted forms. The

* Class A (Farther Series), 1837, p. 91.

keeper informed us they were of several distinct tribes, and that they did not understand one another: this was apparent from the formation of the head. While we were there, five little boys and girls were selected and bought to go into the interior: no regard is paid to relationship, and, once separated, they never meet again! We left the tienda, and, turning through the gateway, we saw some who were lying under the shade of the plantain, whose appearance told that they, at least, would be liberated from bondage by death. They were those who had suffered most during the voyage,—their situation was most melancholy. I offered to one the untasted bowl of cocoa-nut milk I was about drinking,—she motioned it away with a look which, even from a negress, was expressive of thankfulness, and which seemed to say how unused she was to such kindness."

The Quarterly Review (vol. xxx.), contains an article on Mengin's 'Histoire de l'Egypte,'* in which the reviewer, speaking of Ismael Pacha's expedition to the south, says, " The hopes of the Pacha, however, were greatly disappointed in these black troops (captured in Soudan). They were strong, able-bodied men, and not averse from being taught; but when attacked by disease, which soon broke out in the camp, they died like sheep infected with the rot. The medical men ascribed the mor-

* Histoire de l'Egypte par Felix Mengin, 1823.—Quarterly Review, vol. xxx. p. 491.

M

tality to moral rather than physical causes; it appeared in numerous instances, that having been snatched away from their homes and families they were even anxious to get rid of life, and such was the dreadful mortality that ensued, that out of 20,000 of these unfortunate men, 3000 did not remain alive at the end of two years."

Dr. Bowring has stated to me, that the negroes which have been conveyed into Egypt, " suffer much from nostalgia, and when they have been gathered together into regiments, the passionate desire to return home frequently produced a languishing malady, of which they die in large numbers. The mortality among the slaves in Egypt is frightful,—when the epidemical plague visits the country, they are swept away in immense multitudes, and they are the earliest victims of almost every other domineering disease. I have heard it estimated that five or six years are sufficient to sweep away a generation of slaves, at the end of which time the whole has to be replenished. This is one of the causes of their low market-value. When they marry, their descendants seldom live ; in fact, the laws of nature seem to repel the establishment of hereditary slavery."

But it is needless to multiply instances on this head ; and I shall only further notice a few of the authorities for the amount of the mortality after landing, and in the seasoning.

Mr. Pitt, in the debate on the Slave Trade, in

1791, made the following observation—" The evidence before the House, as to this point (the mortality), was perfectly clear; for it would be found in that dreadful catalogue of deaths in consequence of the seasoning and the middle passage, which the House had been condemned to look into, that *one-half* die."

Mr. Wilberforce, in his letter of 1807, (page 98,) says, " The survivors were landed in such a diseased state, that 4½ per cent. of the whole number imported, were estimated to die in the short interval between the arrival of the ship and the sale of the cargo, probably not more than a fortnight; and after the slaves had passed into the hands of the planters, the numbers which perished from the effects of the voyage were allowed to be very considerable." It ought not to be forgotten, that Pitt and Wilberforce are speaking of a period when the Slave Trade was legal, and the Slave Carrying Act in operation. What then may be the *increase* of this mortality, now that the trade is clandestine, and the slaves packed on board of the " Clippers," like " bales of goods ?"

The Duc de Broglie, when addressing the Chamber of Peers on this subject, in March 1822, made the following remark—" And it is a well-known fact, that a *fourth*, or even a *third*, of the cargo generally perishes either on ship-board, or soon after the landing, from the diseases incident to the voyage."*

* Afr. Inst. Report, Ap. 2, No. 16, 1823.

In the debate of 1791, Mr. Stanley (then agent for the Islands and advocating the continuance of the Slave Trade) said, speaking of the negroes—" As to their treatment in the West Indies, he was himself witness that it was in general highly indulgent and humane," and yet " he confessed that ONE-HALF, very frequently, died in the SEASONING."

I have now, in the discharge of a most painful duty, brought under review a complication of human misery and suffering, which I may venture to say has no parallel; but before concluding this branch of the case, it may be proper to exhibit, in a summary manner, the amount of negro mortality, consequent on the Slave Trade.

SUMMARY.

1st. The loss incident to the seizure, march to the coast, and detention there.

Newton (p. 73) is of opinion, that the captives reserved for sale, are fewer than the slain.

Mr. Miles (p. 73) stated to the Committee in 1790, that in one of the " Skirmishes" for slaves, " above sixty thousand men" were destroyed.

Bosman narrates, that in two of these skirmishes " above one hundred thousand men were killed;" and Mr. Devaynes has said, that in one of these " skirmishes " " 60,000 lost their lives."* And Denham (p. 74) narrates, that in five marauding ex-

---

* It is obvious that these very large numbers must be received with considerable qualification. There can be no doubt, however, that the slaughter was great.

cursions, " 20,000 at least," were slaughtered, and 16,000 sent into slavery; and he gives another instance, where " probably 6000 " were slaughtered, in procuring 3000 slaves.

On the route to the coast, we may cite the authority of Park, Denham, &c.; and M. Mendez (p. 87) estimates the loss on this head, to amount to five-twelfths of the whole.

For the mortality occasioned by detention before embarkation, we have the authority of Frazer, Park, Leonard, Landers, and Bailey.

From these authorities, we are fairly entitled to assume that from the sources—seizure, march, and detention, *for every slave embarked, one life is sacrificed.*

2ndly. The loss from the middle passage appears to be *not less than* 25 *per cent.* For this there is conclusive evidence. The witnesses have no assignable motive for exaggeration; they are men holding public situations, of unimpeachable veracity, and with the best opportunities of forming a correct estimate.

The Rev. John Newton had, himself, been for many years a slave-trader, and speaks of what he saw. The Slave trade was then legal, and the vessels employed were usually large and commodious, and very different from the American clippers now in use. He rates the loss during the mid-passage at 25 per cent. Captain Ramsay had commanded one of H. M. cruisers, employed in suppressing the Slave Trade, had taken many slavers, and could not be ignorant of the state of the captured cargoes. His estimate is 33 per cent.

Slave-trading vessels are continually passing under the eye of the Governor of Cape Coast Castle. His attention has been constantly kept alive to the subject, and few men have had such opportunities of arriving at the real truth. Mr. Maclean's estimate is thirty-three per cent.

Commodore Owen reports that which came to his knowledge while he was employed by government in surveying the eastern coast of Africa. His estimate is fifty per cent. This excess, as compared with the others, is accounted for, by the additional length of the voyage round the Cape of Good Hope.

If, after such testimony, there were room for hesitation, it must be removed by witnesses of a very different kind. The Spanish slave-merchants of Monte Video, it is fair to presume, are well acquainted with the usual rate of mortality in their slave-vessels; and we may give them credit for not acting contrary to their own interests; so confident are they that, at least, one-third will perish, that they providently incur the expense of sending out that amount of surplus, for the purpose (in their own words) "of covering the deaths on the voyage."

I should be justified in taking the average of these authorities, which would be thirty-four per cent; but as it is my wish to be assuredly within the mark, I will state the mortality from the middle passage at *twenty-five per cent.*

In the same spirit I will take no notice of the mortality after capture, which, says the report of the Parliamentary Committee, amounts to from one-sixth to one-half.

3dly. As to the loss after landing, and in the seasoning.

Under this head, we have, among others, two authorities which require particular attention ; one of them referring to the time when the Slave Trade was legal, the other to a recent date, and both of them coming from unexceptionable quarters. Mr. Stanley, a West India Agent, arguing for the continuance of the Slave Trade, and lauding the treatment of the negroes, confesses that *one-half* frequently die in the seasoning. The other, the report of the Medical Officers appointed to investigate the state of the liberated Africans at the Gambia ; which describes a large proportion of them as labouring under disease, " nothing equal to which has been known hitherto in the annals of physic." If such be their state when they fall into the hands of the British, are treated by them with kindness, and are relieved from their most frightful apprehensions, may we not suppose that their state is still more miserable, and the mortality still greater, when they are landed clandestinely at Cuba, and know that they are doomed to interminable bondage ?

Upon the strength and authority of these facts, I

might fairly estimate the loss under this head at one-third; but I think I cannot err, on the side of exaggeration, in setting it down at *twenty per cent.*

Nor does the mortality stop here. In slave countries, but more especially where the Slave Trade prevails, there is, invariably, a great diminution of human life; the numbers annually born, fall greatly below the numbers which perish. It would not be difficult to prove, that in the last fifty years there has been, in this way, a waste of millions of lives; but as this view of the subject would involve the horrors of slavery, as well as of the Slave Trade, I shall abstain from adding anything on this head, to the catalogue of mortality which I have already given.

We have thus brought into a narrow compass the mortality arising from the Slave Trade.

		Per Cent.
1.	Seizure, march and detention	100
2.	Middle passage, and after capture	25
3.	After landing, and in the seasoning	20
		145

So that for every 1000 negroes alive at the end of a year after their deportation, and available to the planter, we have a sacrifice of 1450.

Let us apply this calculation to the number landed annually in Cuba, Brazil, &c., which, as I have already shown (p. 26) may be fairly rated at 150,000; of these 20 per cent, or 30,000, die in the seasoning, leaving 120,000 available for the planter.

If 150,000 were landed, there must have been embarked 25 per cent, or 37,500 more, who perish in the passage : and if 187,500 were embarked, 100 per cent, or 187,500 more, must have been sacrificed in the seizure, march, and detention.

It is impossible for any one to reach this result, without suspecting, as well as hoping, that it must be an exaggeration ; and yet there are those who think that this is too low an estimate.*

I have not, however, assumed any fact, without giving the data on which it rests ; neither have I extracted from those data any immoderate inference. I think that the reader, on going over the calculation, will perceive that I have, in almost every instance, abated the deduction, which might with justice have been made. If then we are to put confi-

---

* Mr. Rankin says :—

" The old and new Calebar, the Bonney, Whydah, and the Gallinas, contribute an inexhaustible supply for the French islands of the West Indies, Rio Janeiro, Havana, and the Brazils, where, notwithstanding every opposition and hindrance from the British cruisers, one hundred thousand are supposed to arrive in safety annually ; five times that number having been lost by capture or death. Death thins the cargoes in various modes ; suicide destroys many ; and many are thrown overboard at the close of the voyage ; for as a duty of ten dollars is set by the Brazilian Government upon each slave upon landing, such as seem unlikely to survive, or to bring a price sufficiently high to cover this custom-house tax, are purposely drowned before entering port. Those only escape these wholesale murders who will probably recover health and flesh when removed to the fattening pens of the slave-farmer, a man who contracts to feed up the skeletons to a marketable appearance." Vol. ii. p. 71.

dence in the authorities (most of them official) which
I have quoted, we cannot avoid the conclusion,—terrible as it is,—that the Slave Trade between Africa
and America annually subjects to the horrors of

slavery	120,000
And murders . . . 30,000	
37,500	
187,500	
———	255,000

Annual victims of Christian Slave Trade	375,000
,, ,, of Mohammedan .	100,000.*

Annual loss to Africa . .	475,000

* The following is an estimate of the amount and mortality of
the Northern or Mahommedan Slave Trade :—

Number annually exported by the Imaum of Muscat	30,000
Do. by Traders to Barbary, Egypt, &c. . .	20,000
	50,000

Loss on Seizure, . .	50 per cent	
,, March . .	30 ,,	
,, Detention .	,, ,,	
,, Middle Passage	,, ,,	
Seasoning .	20 ,,	
In all ..	100[1]	
		50,000

Annual victims of Mohammedan Slave Trade	100,000

[1] Dr. Bowring states, (as to Egypt) that 30 per cent. perish in
the first 10 days after seizure; and that the loss from the time of
capture to the arrival at the market in Cairo may be estimated at
100 per cent.

Consequent State of Africa.

Even this is but a part of the total evil. The great evil is, that the Slave Trade exhibits itself in Africa as a barrier, excluding everything which can soften, or enlighten, or civilise, or elevate the people of that vast continent. The Slave Trade suppresses all other trade, creates endless insecurity, kindles perpetual war, banishes commerce, knowledge, social improvement, and above all, Christianity, from one quarter of the globe, and from 100,000,000 of mankind.

Failure of Efforts already made for Suppression of the Slave Trade.

It is but too manifest that the efforts already made for the suppression of the Slave Trade, have not accomplished their benevolent object.

The people of England take a more lively and intense interest in this, than perhaps in any other foreign subject. The Government, whether in the hands of the one party or the other, cannot be accused of having, for a long series of years, been wanting either in zeal, or exertion, for its suppression. Millions of money and multitudes of lives have been sacrificed ; and in return for all, we have only the afflicting conviction, that the Slave Trade is as far as ever from being suppressed. Nay, I am afraid the fact is not to be disputed, that while we have thus been endeavouring to extinguish the traffic, it has actually doubled in amount.

In the debate of 2d April, 1792, Mr. Fox rated the Slave Trade at 80,000 annually : he says, " I think the least disreputable way of accounting for the supply of slaves, is to represent them as having been convicted of crimes by legal authority. What does the House think is the whole number of these convicts exported annually from Africa ? 80,000." In the same debate Mr. Pitt observed, " I know of no evil that ever has existed, nor can imagine any evil to exist, worse than the tearing of 80,000 persons annually from their native land, by a combination of the most civilised nations in the most enlightened quarter of the globe." The late Zachary Macaulay, than whom the African has had no better friend, told me a few days before his death, that upon the most accurate investigation he was able to make as to the extent of the Slave Trade, he had come to the conclusion that it was 70,000 annually, fifty years ago. Twenty years ago the African Institution reported to the Duke of Wellington that it was 70,000. We will assume then that the number at the commencement of the discussion was 70,000 negroes annually transported from Africa. There is evidence before the Parliamentary Committees, to show that about one-third was for the British islands, and one-third for St. Domingo, so that strictly speaking, if the Slave Trade of other countries had been stationary, they ought only at the utmost to import 25,000 ; but I have already proved

that the number annually landed in Cuba and Brazil,
&c., is 150,000, being more than double the whole
draught upon Africa, including the countries where
it had ceased when the Slave Trade controversy
began. Twice as many human beings are now its
victims as when Wilberforce and Clarkson entered
upon their noble task ; and each individual of this
increased number, in addition to the horrors which
were endured in former times, has to suffer from
being cribbed up in a narrower space, and on board
a vessel, where accommodation is sacrificed to speed.
Painful as this is, it becomes still more distressing
if it shall appear that our present system has not
failed by mischance, from want of energy, or from
want of expenditure, but that the system itself is er-
roneous, and must necessarily. be attended with dis-
appointment.

Hitherto we have effected no other change than a
change in the flag under which the trade is carried
on. It was stated by our ambassador at Paris, to the
French minister, in 1824 (I speak from memory),
that the French flag covered the villains of all nations.
For some years afterwards the Spanish flag was generally used. Now, Portugal sells her flag, and the
greater part of the trade is carried on under it. Her
governors openly sell, at a fixed price, the use of
Portuguese papers and flag.

So grave an accusation ought not to be made
without stating some of the authorities on which it
is grounded. In a Parliamentary paper on the

subject of the Slave Trade, presented in 1823, Sir Charles M'Carthy states in his letter of the 19th June 1822,* that " the case of the ' Conde de Ville Flor,' seized near Bissao, fully establishes that Signor Andrade, the governor, had shipped a number of slaves on his own account." Sir Charles further states that " he received repeated reports of the governors of Bissao and Cacheo having full cargoes of slaves in irons ready for all purchasers; and that the traffic is carried on openly at the Cape de Verd Islands, St. Thomas, and Prince's." This statement is confirmed by " Lieutenant Hagan, of Her Majesty's brig Thistle, who informed him that the traffic in slaves was carried on at Bissao and Cacheo in the most open manner, under the sanction of the governor, the latter of whom is the principal dealer in slaves."

The practice of 1822 has continued to the present time. On the 3d March 1838, Lord Palmerston, in a spirited note, states to the Portuguese Minister, " that the Portuguese flag is lent, with the connivance of Portuguese authorities, to serve as a protection for all the miscreants of every other nation in the world, who may choose to engage in such base pursuits."†

The charge thus made, extends only to the *lending* of the flag of Portugal; it might have gone farther. In an enclosure in a letter from Lord Palmerston to

---

* Papers, Slave Trade, 11th July, 1823.

† Class B. (Farther Series), 1837, p. 29, presented 1838.

our Ambassador at Lisbon, dated 30th April 1838, it appears that "the Governor of Angola has established an impost or fee of 700,000 reis to be paid to him for every vessel which embarks slaves from thence, it being understood that upon payment of the above-mentioned sum, no impediment to the illicit trade shall be interposed by the governor, nor any farther risk be incurred by the persons engaged in the trade."* Nor is this all. In the same document we find that the governor, not content with lending and letting out the flag of Portugal, has set up as a slave-trader himself; "sending from Angola, for his own account, a shipment of slaves, sixty in number, which he has consigned to a notorious slave-dealer of the name of Vincente, at Rio de Janeiro."†

It is very truly added, that these violations of the treaties "form but a small portion of the offences of this kind constantly committed by Portuguese subjects, both in and out of authority."

When Portugal shall have been persuaded or compelled to desist from this insulting violation of treaty, it is but too probable that Brazil will step into her place. We find it stated in a despatch from Her Majesty's Commissioners at Rio de Janeiro to Lord Palmerston, of date the 17th November 1837,‡ that "The change in the Brazilian Government which took place on the 19th September, has had this important consequence in respect to the Slave

* Class B. (Farther Series), 1837, p. 35.   † Ibid.
‡ Class A (Farther Series), 1837, p. 80.

Trade, that while the late Government appeared to wish to put down the traffic, as matter of principle, and of compact with Great Britain, the present Government, as far as it is represented by Senior Vasconcellos (Minister of Justice, and provisionally Minister for the empire), has proclaimed the traffic to be indispensable to the country, has released those concerned who were under prosecution; and set at nought the engagement with Great Britain on this head." And the British Consul at Pernambuco writes to Lord Palmerston, of date 15th February 1838, " The editor of the Jornal de Commercio declares, that this important subject has already passed the Senate, and that there is every probability it will be made law in the next Session of the Legislature, to annul the enactment of 17th November 1831, which prohibits the Slave Trade in Brazil under severe penalties."* When Brazil shall be induced to surrender the traffic, it is not improbable that it will be transferred to Buenos Ayres, or one of the many remaining flags of South America; then to Texas; and when we shall have dealt with all these, and shall have wrung from them a reluctant engagement to renounce the iniquity, we shall still have to deal with the United States of North America.

How long, it may be asked, will it take before we have succeeded in gaining from the whole world a concurrence in the provisions of the existing treaty

* Class B (Farther Series), 1837, p. 54.

with Spain? We began our negotiations with Portugal about thirty years ago ; and in what state are they now ? By a despatch from Lord Howard de Walden, our ambassador at Lisbon, to Lord Palmerston, of date 25th February 1838, we are informed, that Viscount de Sa da Bandeira, the Portuguese minister, having been urged to proceed with the negotiations, replied, " That he would do so as soon as he had settled a treaty with Spain for the navigation of the Douro, the negotiation of which occupied his whole time."*

To touch upon one only of the many difficulties which lie in the way of a universal confederacy for putting down the Slave Trade, I ask, how shall we get the consent of North America to the article yielding the right of search. She has told us, in the most peremptory terms, that she will never assent to it ; and it should be remembered, that this confederacy must either be universally binding, or it is of no avail. It will avail us little that ninety-nine doors are closed, if one remains open. To that one outlet, the whole Slave Trade of Africa will rush.

Does any one suppose that even in the space of half a century, we shall have arrived at one universal combination of all countries, for the suppression of the Slave Trade ? And a delay of fifty years, at the present rate of the traffic, implies, at the very least, the slaughter of eleven millions of mankind

* Class B (Farther Series), 1837, p. 30.

N

But let us suppose this combination to have been effected, and that all nations consent to the four leading articles of the Spanish Treaty. When that is done, it will be unavailing.

In the first place, during the three years which have elapsed since the treaty with Spain, the Slave Trade has been carried on by the Spaniards, at least to as great an extent as formerly. On the 2d January 1836, the Commissioners at Sierra Leone say, "There is nothing in the experience of the past year to show that the Slave Trade with Spain has, in any degree, diminished."*

The Commissioners at the Havanah say, "Never has the Slave Trade at the Havanah reached such a disgraceful pitch as during the year 1835."† I could corroborate this statement, that there is no diminution in the Spanish Slave Trade, by a variety of letters. One gentleman, upon whose sources of information and accuracy I can entirely rely, says, in a letter dated September 1836, "the Slave Trade, which was thought to be dead here some years ago, has still a mighty being, and stalks over the island in all its pristine audacity." Another, of date November 1836, says, "Article first of the late Treaty between England and Spain states, 'The Slave Trade is hereby declared, on the part of Spain, to be henceforward totally and finally abolished in all parts of the world.' In answer to this, we assert that the Slave Trade carried on by the Spaniards is

* Class A, 1835, p. 9.   † Ibid. p. 206.

more brisk than ever. In December 1836, a gentleman, detained a month at St. Jago de Cuba, witnessed the arrival of five slave cargoes from Africa."

But it may be said that this arises from the facility with which the Portuguese flag is obtained, and that when Portugal, and all other powers, shall have consented to the Spanish Treaty, this mode of evasion will have ceased. It is perfectly true that the Portuguese flag is obtained with the greatest facility at a very moderate price. At the Cape de Verd Islands, at the River Cacheo, at St. Thomas', at Prince's, and at Angola, the Portuguese flag may be easily and cheaply purchased. But notwithstanding, we find by the last parliamentary papers, that out of the twenty-seven vessels condemned at Sierra Leone, *eight* were under the Spanish flag; and of the seventy-two vessels which left the port of Havanah for the coast of Africa, in 1837, no fewer than *nineteen* at least were *Spanish.** The slave-traders surely did not think that the Spanish Treaty was a death-blow to the trade, or they would not have neglected the precaution of purchasing, at a very easy price, the protection afforded by the flag of Portugal.

They had their choice of the Spanish flag, attended by all the dangers supposed to arise from the Spanish Treaty, or the Portuguese flag, which is not liable to these dangers; and for the sake of saving a very trivial sum, they prefer the former.

But there is another mode of measuring the im-

* Class A (Farther Series), 1837, p. 68.

portance which the slave-traders attach to the Spanish Treaty. The Commissioners, in their Report of 1836, after stating that the first effect of the treaty was to arrest the Slave Trade, add, that this alarm soon wore away, and " now the only visible effect of the reported new treaty is an increased rate of premium out and home, with an augmented price of negroes."*

The Spanish Treaty has been for some time a topic of continual congratulation and complacency; and there are many who think that if we could but induce Portugal and other countries to follow the example of Spain, there would be an end of the Slave Trade. A case occurs in the papers presented to Parliament in 1838, which throws a strong light on the real efficacy of the Spanish Treaty; and, though I can give but a scanty outline of it here, it deserves particular attention. The Vincedora, a Spanish vessel, officered by Spaniards, having lately returned from a trading voyage to Africa, came into the port of Cadiz, bound for Porto Rico. At Cadiz she took in forty-nine passengers, and proceeded on her way. The passengers suffered considerable annoyance from the effluvia proceeding from the lower parts of the ship. By this, and by other circumstances, some vague suspicion seems to have been engendered. Leaving Porto Rico, the vessel proceeded towards Cuba; on her way thither she fell in with the Ringdove, Captain Nixon. The

* Class A, 1835, p. 207

captain of the Vincedora denied that he had negroes on board; but the mate of the Ringdove insisted on pursuing his search, and in the forepeak of the vessel, closed up from light or air, were found twenty-six negroes;* " most of them were young, from ten years old upwards."

They could not speak one word of Spanish, unless it be true, which the Spanish witnesses labour hard to prove, that one of them was once heard to use the word " Senor." From these circumstances, from the stench perceived by the passengers after leaving Cadiz; from the fact of three iron coppers being found, and large quantities of rice and Indian corn having daily been dressed in them ; from the care taken to debar the passengers from all access to those parts of the ship where they were found; and from the testimony, through an interpreter, of the negroes themselves, " who all declared, most solemnly, that they had never been in another vessel, and swore to it, after the manner of their country;" from all these circumstances it is clear (however incredible the atrocity) that these wretches had been shipped at Congo, in Africa, had been carried across the Atlantic to Cadiz, again across the Atlantic to Porto Rico, and were, when taken, in the progress of a third voyage.

No record exists of the number originally shipped,

---

* They appeared to be of recent importation, had no other clothing than a piece of cloth tied round their loins, their heads were shaven, and some of them were in a sad state of emaciation. Class A, 1837, p. 40.

nor of those who were so happy as to perish by the way, nor of the extent of misery undergone by those who endured a voyage from Africa to Europe, and from Europe to America, of not less than 6000 miles, pining in their narrow, loathsome, and sultry prison, for want of air, and light, and water. These particulars will never be known in this world; but who will deny that the English captain is justified in calling it a case of " utter barbarity?" He might have added, of " utter perfidy." In a private letter, he says, — " The Vincedora took her wretched cargo round by Cadiz (can you conceive such barbarity?), and there got armed with government authority as a packet, wearing the royal colours and pendant; they (the slavers) will be liberated, and I may be prosecuted." The fact of her having slaves on board must have been known to the custom-house authorities at Cadiz.

However, thanks to the Spanish Treaty, the ship is captured at last, and the Spanish authorities will be, of course, as eager as ourselves to punish the villain who has thus defied her decrees. Captain Nixon took his prize to the Havanah, and she was tried before the Mixed Commission Court. The captain of the slaver set up the impudent defence— First, that these naked, filthy, shaven, emaciated creatures, were " passengers," and, next, that they were " parcels of goods from Porto Rico."

The court, by the casting vote of the Spanish umpire, found this false and flimsy pretext valid, acquitted

the slaver, restored the vessel, and condemned the innocent negroes to slavery, while Captain Nixon is exposed to heavy damages for doing his duty! The
captain of the Vincedora is triumphant, and, in a
complaint which he made relating to certain articles
which, as he alleges, are missing, closes the scene by a
high-flown address to the court, on "the faith of
treaties," " the sacred rights of property and national
decorum," and "the outraged honour of the respected
flag of England !"

Worse than all is the fact that this case has been
taken as a precedent, and already another vessel, the
Vigilante, has been liberated on the strength of this
decision.

Had I fabricated a case to show the perfidy of the
Spanish authorities, and the barefaced evasions, which
are sufficient, in Lord Palmerston's words, " to reduce
the treaty to mere waste paper," I could scarcely have
produced one so much to the purpose.

I am compelled to go further. It may be pretended that it was only by accident that the slaver,
while she remained at Cadiz, escaped the vigilance
of the custom-house officers, and by a second fortunate accident that she obtained permission to bear
the royal pendant ; but can it also be ascribed to accident, that the two persons selected by the Spanish
Government as commissioner and arbitrator should
have acted throughout as if their proper business was
to defend the slave-trader, and defeat the treaty ? It
would seem that, while hardly any evidence is strong

enough to convict a slaver, no pretext is too miserable for his defence. For example, the Vincedora is declared to. be " wrongfully detained," while the General Laborde, " a well-known and fully-equipped slaver," is liberated " because the wife and children of the supercargo were on board."*

Upon the whole, I can arrive at no other conclusion than that the Spanish Treaty, as interpreted by the Spanish judges, is an impudent fraud; and that those who shall be credulous enough to rely upon it for the full attainment of our object will be fatally deceived.

Thus, then, stands the argument : we shall never obtain the concurrence of all the powers to the provisions of the Spanish Treaty; and if we get it, we shall find it not worth having. But even assuming that those insurmountable obstacles have been overcome, and that the Spanish Treaty, improved and rendered more stringent, becomes the law of the civilised world; it will still appear that this treaty will not accomplish our object. Another step must be taken; and the next step will be to make slave-trading PIRACY punishable with death.

Once more, then, we shall have to tread the tedious round of negotiation. To say nothing of the difficulty we shall find in inducing Portugal to adopt the greater measure, when she has so long refused to take the minor step; and nothing of the difficulty

* Class A, 1837 p. 91.

of persuading Brazil to advance, when she has exhibited unequivocal symptoms of a disposition to retreat; nor of the reluctance of Spain, (who thinks she has conceded too much,) to make still farther concessions—to say nothing of all these, France stands in our way. She has declared that by her constitution, it cannot be made piracy.

I am afraid that there is not the remotest probability of inducing all nations to concur in so strong a measure, as that of stigmatising the Slave Trade as piracy.

But we will suppose all these difficulties removed; a victory in imagination has been obtained over the pride of North America, the cupidity of Portugal, the lawlessness of Texas, and the constitution of France. Let it be granted that the Spanish Treaty, with an article for piracy, has become universal. I maintain that the Slave Trade, even then, will not be put down. Three nations have already tried the experiment of declaring the Slave Trade to be piracy—Brazil, North America, and England. Brazilian subjects, from the time of passing the law have been continually engaged in the Slave Trade; indeed we are informed that the whole population of certain districts are concerned in it, and *not one* has suffered under the law of piracy. In 1820, a law was passed by the legislature of North America, declaring that if any citizen of that country shall be engaged in the Slave Trade, " such citizen or person shall be adjudged a pirate, and on conviction thereof, before the

Circuit Court of the United States, shall suffer death." It will not be denied, that American citizens have been largely engaged in the traffic ; but I have yet to learn that even one capital conviction has taken place during the eighteen years that have elapsed since the law was passed.*

Great Britain furnishes a still more striking illustration of the inefficacy of such a law. For ten years, the Slave Trade prevailed at the Mauritius, to use the words of Captain Moresby, before the Committee of the House of Commons, " as plain as the sun at noonday." Many were taken in the very act, and yet no conviction, I believe, took place. With these examples before me, I am not so sanguine as some other gentlemen appear to be, as to the efficacy of a law declaring the Slave Trade piracy, even if it were universally adopted. I fear that such a law would be a dead letter, unless, at all events, we had the *bonâ fide* and cordial co-operation of the colonists. Were we able to obtain this in our own dominions ? Our naval officers acted with their usual energy, on the coast of the Mauritius. When General Hall was governor there, and when Mr. Edward Byam was the head of

---

* Major M'Gregor has stated, in the letter to which I have before referred, that a vessel, with 160 Africans on board, had been wrecked at the Bahamas; and he says, " This pretended Portuguese vessel was fitted out at Baltimore, United States, having been formerly a pilot-boat, called the Washington. The supercargo was an American citizen from Baltimore." See also the report of the Commissioners, Class B, 1837, p. 125.

the police, everything possible was done to suppress the traffic, and to bring the criminals to justice. No persons could act with more meritorious fidelity (and I grieve to say, poorly have they been rewarded, by the Home Government) ; it became, however, but too evident that the law was unavailing. The populace would not betray the slave-trader, the agent of the police would not seize him; if captured by our officers, the prisons would not hold him, and the courts would not convict him. General Hall was obliged to resort to the strong expedient of sending offenders of this kind to England, for trial at the Old Bailey, on the ground that no conviction could be obtained on the island. It is clear, then, that the law making Slave Trade piracy, will be unavailing, without you obtain the concurrence of the colonists in Cuba and Brazil ; and who is so extravagant as to indulge the hope that this will ever be attained ?

But now I will make a supposition, still more Utopian than any of the preceding. All nations shall have acceded to the Spanish Treaty, and that treaty shall be rendered more effective. They shall have linked to it, the article of piracy ; the whole shall have been clenched, by the cordial concurrence of the authorities at home, and the populace in the colonies. With all this, we shall be once more defeated and baffled by contraband trade.

The power which will overcome our efforts, is the *extraordinary profit* of the slave-trader. It is, I believe, an axiom at the Custom-house, that no illicit trade can be suppressed, where the profits exceed 30 per cent.

I will prove that the profits of the slave-trader are nearly five times that amount. "Of the enormous profits of the Slave Trade," says Commissioner Macleay, "the most correct idea will be formed by taking an example. The last vessel condemned by the Mixed Commission was the Firm." He gives the cost of—

	Dollars.
Her cargo . .	28,000
Provisions, ammunition, wear and tear, &c. .	10,600
Wages . . .	13,400
Total expense . .	52,000
Total product . .	145,000*

There was a clear profit on the human cargo of this vessel, of 18,640*l.*, or just 180 per cent.; and will any one who knows the state of Cuba and Brazil, pretend that this is not enough to shut the mouth of the informer, to arrest the arm of the police, to blind the eyes of the magistrates, and to open the doors of the prison ?

Lord Howard de Walden, in a despatch to the Duke of Wellington, dated 26th February, 1835, speaks of a vessel just about to sail from that port (Lisbon), on a slave-trading voyage. It shows the kind of reliance which we are justified in placing on

* Parl. Paper, No. 381, p. 37.

the professions of that country, pledged twenty years ago, "to co-operate with His Britannic Majesty in the cause of humanity and justice," and "to extend the blessings of peaceful industry and innocent commerce to Africa;" when, in her own capital, under the guns of her own forts, in the face of day, and before the eyes of our ambassador, a vessel is permitted, without molestation, to embark in the Slave Trade; but it also exhibits the prodigious gains of the man merchant.

Lord Howard de Walden says, "The subject of her departure and destination have become quite notorious, and the sum expected to be cleared by the parties concerned in the enterprise, is put at 40,000*l.*"*

Mr. Maclean, (Governor at Cape Coast Castle,) in a letter addressed to me, in May, 1838, says, " A prime slave on that part of the coast with which I have most knowledge, costs about 50 dollars in goods, or about from 25 to 30 dollars in money, including prime cost and charges; the same slave will sell in Cuba for 350 dollars readily, but from this large profit must be deducted freight, insurance, commission, cost of feeding during the middle passage, and incidental charges, which will reduce the net profit to, I should say, 200 dollars on each prime slave; and this must be still further reduced, to make up for casualties, to, perhaps, 150 dollars per head."

It is remarkable that this calculation by Mr. Maclean almost exactly corresponds with that stated by

* Class B, 1835, p. 27.

the Sierra Leone Commissioners, giving for the outlay of 100 dollars, a return of 280 dollars.

Once more, then, I must declare my conviction that the Trade will never be suppressed by the system hitherto pursued.* You will be defeated by its enormous gains. You may throw impediments in the way of these miscreants; you may augment their peril; you may reduce their profits; but enough, and more than enough, will remain to baffle all your humane efforts.

* Mr. Maclean, in a letter dated 16th October, 1838, says, " My neighbour (as I may call him), De Souza, at Whydah, still carries on an extensive Slave Trade ; judging by the great number of vessels consigned to him, he must ship a vast number of slaves annually. He declares, and with truth, that all the slave treaties signed during the last 25 years, have never caused him to export one slave fewer than he would have done otherwise."

COMMERCIAL INTERCOURSE WITH AFRICA.

"It was not possible for me to behold the fertility of the soil, the vast herds of cattle, proper both for labour and food, and a variety of other circumstances favourable to colonization and agriculture, and reflect withal on the means which presented themselves of a vast inland navigation, without lamenting that a country so abundantly gifted and honoured by nature, should remain in its present savage and neglected state."—Park.

"It is more than probable, as we have now ascertained that a water communication may be carried on with so extensive a part of the interior of Africa, that a considerable trade will be opened with the country through which we have passed. The natives only require to know what is wanted of them, and to be shown what they will have in return, and much produce which is now lost from neglect, will be turned to a considerable account."—Lander.

"The commercial intercourse of Africa opens an inexhaustible source of wealth to the manufacturing interests of Great Britain—to all which the Slave Trade is a physical obstruction."—Gustavus Vasa. *Letter to Lord Hawkesbury*, 1788.

Our system hitherto has been to obtain the co-operation of European powers, while we have paid very little attention to what might be done in Africa itself, for the suppression of the Slave Trade. Our efforts in that direction have been few, faint, and limited to isolated spots, and those by no means well chosen. To me it appears that the converse of this policy would have offered greater probabilities of success; that, while no reasonable expectations can be entertained of overturning this gigantic evil through the agency and with the concurrence of the civilised world, there is a well-founded hope, amounting almost to a certainty, that this object may be attained through the medium and with the concurrence of Africa herself. If, instead of our expensive and fruitless negotiations with Portugal, we had been, during the last twenty years, engaged in extending our intercourse with the nations of Africa, unfolding to them the capabilities of her soil, and the inexhaustible store of wealth which human labour might derive from its cultivation, and convincing them that the Slave Trade alone debars them from enjoying a vastly more affluent supply of our valuable commodities, and if we had leagued ourselves with them to suppress that baneful traffic, which is their enemy even more than it is ours, there is reason to believe that Africa would not have been what Africa is, in spite of all our exertions,—one universal den of desolation, misery, and crime.

Why do I despair of winning the hearty co-operation of those European powers who now encourage or connive at the Slave Trade ? I answer, because we have no sufficient bribe to offer. The secret of their resistance is the 180 per cent. profit which attaches to the Slave Trade. This is a temptation which we cannot outbid. It has been, and it will be, the source of their persevering disregard of the claims of humanity, and of their contempt for the engagements, however solemn, which they have contracted with us.

But why do I entertain a confident persuasion that

we may obtain the cordial concurrence of the African powers? Because the Slave Trade is not their gain, but their loss. It is their ruin, because it is capable of demonstration, that, but for the Slave Trade, the other trade of Africa would be increased fifty or a hundred-fold. Because central Africa now receives in exchange for all her exports, both of people and productions, less than half a million of imports, one-half of which may be goods of the worst description, and a third made up of arms and ammunition. What a wretched return is this, for the productions of so vast, so fertile, so magnificent a territory! Take the case of central Africa; the insignificance of our trade with it is forcibly exhibited by contrasting the whole return from thence with some single article of no great moment which enters Great Britain. The feathers received at Liverpool from Ireland reach an amount exceeding all the productions of central Africa; the eggs from France and Ireland exceed one-half of it; while the value of pigs from Ireland into the port of Liverpool is three times as great as the whole trade of Great Britain in the productions of the soil of central Africa.*   What an exhibition does

	£.
* Eggs, total amount unknown, but into London, Liverpool, and Glasgow, from France and Ireland alone	275,000
Feathers from Ireland to Liverpool (Porter's "Progress of Nation," p. 83) . .	500,000
Pigs from Ireland to Liverpool (Porter, Ibid.)	1,488,555
Total imports, productions of the soil of Central Africa (Porter's Tables, Supplement, No. 5)	456,014

this give of the ruin which the Slave Trade entails on Africa! Can it be doubted that, with the extinction of that blight there would arise up a commerce which would pour into Africa, European articles of a vastly superior quality, and to a vastly superior amount?

If it be true that Africa would be enriched, and that her population would enjoy, in multiplied abundance, those commodities, for the acquisition of which she now incurs such intense misery, the one needful thing, in order to induce them to unite with us in repressing the Slave Trade, is, to convince them that they will gain by selling the productive labour of the people, instead of the people themselves.

My first object, then, is to show that Africa possesses within herself the means of obtaining, by fair trade, a greater quantity of our goods than she now receives from the Slave Trade; and, secondly, to point out how this truth may be made plain to the African nations. I have farther to prove, that Great Britain, and other countries (for the argument applies as much to them as to us), have an interest in the question only inferior to that of Africa, and that if we cannot be persuaded to suppress the Slave Trade for the fear of God, or in pity to man, it ought to be done for the lucre of gain.

The importance of Africa, as a vast field of European commerce, though it has been frequently adverted to, and its advantages distinctly pointed out, by those who have visited that part of the world, has not hitherto sufficiently engaged public attention, or led to any great practical results. It is, perhaps, not difficult to account for the apathy which has been manifested on this subject—Africa has a bad name; its climate is represented, and not altogether unjustly, as pestilential, and destructive of European life ; its population as barbarous and ignorant, indolent and cruel—more addicted to predatory warfare than to the arts of peace ; and its interior as totally inaccessible to European enterprise. With the exception of a few spots, such as Sierra Leone, the Gambia, the Senegal, &c., its immensely extended line of coast is open to the ravages and demoralization of the Slave Trade, and the devastating incursions of pirates. The difficulties connected with the establishment of a legitimate commerce with Africa, may be traced principally to these circumstances; and could they be removed, by the removal of their cause, the obstacles arising from climate—the supposed character of its people—and the difficulty of access to the interior, would be easily overcome.

A legitimate commerce with Africa would put down the Slave Trade, by demonstrating the superior value of man as a labourer on the soil, to man as an object of merchandise ; and if conducted on wise and equitable principles, might be the precursor, or rather the attendant, of civilization, peace, and Christianity, to the unenlightened, warlike, and heathen tribes who now so fearfully prey on each other, to supply the slave-markets of the New World. In this view of the subject, the merchant, the philanthropist, the patriot, and the Christian, may unite ; and should the Government of this country lend its powerful influence in organising a commercial system on just, liberal, and comprehensive principles—guarding the rights of the native on the one hand, and securing protection to the honest trader on the other,—a blow would be struck at the nefarious traffic in human beings, from which it could not recover ; and the richest blessings would be conferred on Africa, so long desolated and degraded by its intercourse with the basest and most iniquitous part of mankind.

The present condition of Africa in relation to commerce is deplorable.

The whole amount of goods exported direct from Great Britain to all Africa is considerably within one million sterling.

In the year 1835, the declared value of British and Irish produce and manufactures exported to the whole of Africa was £917,726.

Central Africa possesses within itself everything from which commerce springs. No country in the world has nobler rivers, or more fertile soil ; and it contains a population of fifty millions.

This country, which ought to be amongst the chief of our customers, takes from us only to the value of £312,938 of our manufactures, £101,104* of which are made up of the value of arms and ammunition, and lead and shot.

* Parliamentary Returns for 1837.

I must request the reader to fix his attention on these facts; they present a dreadful picture of the moral prostration of Africa,—of the power of the Slave Trade in withering all healthy commerce,—of the atrocious means resorted to, in order to maintain and perpetuate its horrors,—and of the very slender sum which can be put down as expended in fair and honest trading.

The declared value of British and Irish produce and manufactures, exported in 1837, was, according to parliamentary returns—

To Asia	.	.	.	£993,019
America	.	.	.	15,496,552
Australia	.	.	.	921,568
Hayti	.	.	.	171,050
Central Africa	.	.		312,938

Deducting from this last sum the value of arms, ammunition, &c., the remnant of the annual trade of this country, so favoured by nature, and endowed with such capabilities for commerce, is but £211,834.

There is many a cotton-spinner in Manchester who manufactures much more; there are some dealers in London whose yearly trade is ten times that sum; and there is many a merchant in this country, who exports more than the amount of our whole exports to Africa, arms and ammunition included.

The imports from Africa into this country, though they have, undoubtedly, increased since the year

1820, are still extremely limited; and it is observable that they scarcely embrace any articles, the result of the cultivation of the soil. Their estimated value, in 1834, was 456,014*l*.* (exclusive of gold dust, about 260,000*l*.); they consisted chiefly of palm-oil, teak timber, gums, ivory, bees'-wax, &c., all extremely valuable, and in great demand, but obtained at comparatively little labour and cost.

So small an amount of exports from a country so full of mineral and vegetable wealth, either shows the extreme ignorance and indolence of the people, or the total want of security both to person and property which exists in consequence of the Slave Trade. All the authorities which are accessible clearly show that the latter is the true cause why the commerce between Africa and the civilised world is so trifling; and there is one remarkable fact which corroborates it, namely, that nearly all the legitimate trade with central Africa, is effected through the medium of those stations which have been established by the British and French governments on its coasts, and in, and around which, the trade in slaves has either been greatly checked, or has totally disappeared.

But limited as the commerce of Africa is at present with the civilised world, and infamous as one part of that commerce has been, it is capable of being indefinitely increased, and of having a character impressed on it, alike honourable to all parties engaged in it. The advantages which would accrue to Africa,

* See Porter's Tables.

in the development of her resources, the civilization of her people, and the destruction of one of the greatest evils which has ever afflicted or disgraced mankind,—not less than the benefits which would be secured to Europe in opening new marts for her produce and new fields for her commercial enterprise, would be incalculable.

1. Its geographical position and contiguity to Europe claim for it especial attention. The voyage from the port of London to the Senegal is generally accomplished in twenty-five days; to the Gambia in twenty-eight or thirty days; to Sierra Leone, in thirty to thirty-five days; to Cape Coast Castle, in forty-two to forty-eight days; to Fernando Po, forty-eight to fifty-three days; to the ports in the Bight of Biafra, in fifty to fifty-five days; to the Zaire or Congo, in fifty-five to sixty days, respectively. Vessels leaving Bristol or Liverpool for the same ports possess an advantage, in point of time, of from five to eight days. The voyage is attended with little danger, provided common care be used. The homeward voyage is of course considerably longer than the outward, in consequence of the vessels being obliged to take, what is commonly called, the western passage, having generally to go as far as 40° west longitude. The difference in the length of the voyages, outward and homeward, may be stated at from three to four weeks.

The use of steam would, of course, greatly diminish the length of the voyage, and facilitate the operations of the trader, until establishments could be formed to which the produce required might be conveyed by the natives.

The best season for visiting the African coast is the *dry* season, that is, from December to May. But it may be remarked that the line of coast from Cape Palmas to Cape St. Paul's is less subject to rains than the Windward Coast or the Bights, and may be visited at any season. The worst period of the year is from the middle of July to the middle of December.*

2. Its natural productions† and commercial resources are inexhaustible. From the testimony of

---

* The chief causes of the sickness and mortality on board trading vessels may be ascribed, first, to climate, second, to overwork, and especially exposure to the action of the sun while working; and third, to drunkenness. This last is the chief cause of mortality. One great means of preventing sickness would be, to make it imperative for all trading-vessels to employ a certain number of natives, as is done on board men-of-war.

Mr. Becroft (a merchant who resided for a number of years at Fernando Po) went up the Niger in the Quorra steam-boat, on a trading voyage, in 1836; his expedition lasted three months. He had with him a crew of forty persons, including five white men. Only one individual died, a white man, who was previously far gone in consumption.

† PRODUCTIONS.—*Animals.*—Oxen, sheep, goats, pigs, &c. &c., Guinea fowls, common poultry, ducks, &c.

Grain.—Rice, Indian corn, Guinea corn, or millet, &c.

Fruits.—Oranges, lemons, guavas, pines, citrons, limes, papaws, plantains, bananas, &c. &c.

Roots.—Manioc, igname, batalee, yams, arrow-root, ginger, sweet potato, &c. &c.

Timber.—Teak, ebony, lignum vitæ, and forty or fifty other species of wood for all purposes.

Nuts.—Palm-nut, shea-nut, cocoa-nut, cola-nut, ground-nut, castor-nut, netta-nut, &c. &c.

Dyes.

merchants whose enterprise has, for many years past, led them to embark capital in the African trade ; and from the evidence furnished by the journals of travellers into the interior of the country,* we gather

Dyes.—Carmine, yellow various shades, blue, orange various shades, red, crimson, brown, &c.

Dye woods.—Cam-wood, bar-wood, &c. &c.

Gums.—Copal, Senegal, mastic, sudan, &c.

Drugs.—Aloes, cassia, senna, frankincense, &c.

Minerals.—Gold, iron, copper, emery, sal-ammoniac, nitre, &c.

Sugar-cane, coffee, cotton, indigo, tobacco, India rubber, bees'-wax, ostrich feathers and skins, ivory, &c.

Fish.—Of an immense variety, and in great abundance.

NOTE.—The above is a very imperfect list, but it may serve to show, at a glance, some of the riches of Africa. For all the statements relating to Africa, its capabilities and productions, I have specific authorities ; but it seems hardly necessary to quote them.

* I shall here mention some of the names of countries and kingdoms :—

Timbuctoo, the great emporium of trade in central Africa.

The powerful kingdom of *Gago*, 400 Arabic miles from Timbuctoo to the south-east, abounds with corn and cattle. *Guber*, to the east of Gago, abounds with cattle. *Cano*, once the famous Ghana, abounds with corn, rice, and cattle. *Cashna, Agadez*, fields abound with rice, millet, and cotton. *Guangara*, south of this, a region greatly abounding in gold and aromatics. *Balia*, celebrated for its fine gold, four months' voyage to Timbuctoo. *Bournou*, its capital very large, and inhabitants great traders. The country very rich and fertile, and produces rice, beans, cotton, hemp, indigo in abundance, horses, buffaloes, and horned cattle, sheep, goats, camels, &c. *Yaoorie* produces abundance of rice. The country between *R. Formosa* and *Adra* affords the finest prospect in the world. Inland it is healthy, and the climate good. Trees uncommonly large and beautiful, cotton of the finest quality amazingly plentiful, and indigo and other dye stuffs abundant. The *Jabboos* carry on great trade in grain between *Benin and Lagos*. *Boossa* is a large emporium for trade. The place where

that Nature has scattered her bounties with the most lavish hand ; and that what is required to make them available to the noblest purposes is a legitimate commerce sustained by the government, and directed by honourable men.

In the animal kingdom, I find that in addition to the wild beasts which infest its forests, and occupy its swamps, and whose skins, &c., are valuable as an article of commerce, immense herds of cattle, incalculable in number, range its plains. Hides, therefore, to almost any amount, may be obtained ; and well-fed beef, of excellent quality and flavour, can be

the people from the sea-coast meet the caravans from Barbary to exchange their merchandise. From Boossa to Darfur, there are numerous powerful, fertile, cultivated, well-wooded, watered, populous, and industrious states. Benin, Bournou, Dar Saley, Darfur, Kashua, Houssa, Timbuctoo, Sego, Wassenah, and many others, are populous kingdoms, abounding in metals, minerals, fruits, grain, cattle, &c.

Attah, on the Niger, healthy, many natural advantages, will be a place of great importance, alluvial soil, &c. The places on the banks of the Niger rich in sheep, goats, bullocks, &c.

Fundah, population 30,000 ; beautiful country.

Doma, population large and industrious.

Beeshle and Jacoba, places of great trade.

Rabba, population 40,000.

Toto, population immense.

Alorie (Feletah), vast herds and flocks.

Bumbum, thoroughfare for merchants, from Houssa, Borgoo, &c., to Gonga, vast quantity of land cultivated.

Gungo (Island), palm-trees in profusion.

Egga, two miles in length ; vast number of canoes. Egga to Bournou, said to be fifteen days' journey.

Tschadda, on its banks immense herds of elephants seen, from 50 to 400 at a time.

obtained at some of our settlements, at from 2*d.* to 3*d.* per lb. There are also in various districts immense flocks of sheep ; but as they are covered with a very coarse wool, approaching to hair, and their flesh is not very good on the coast, it may be said, that though numerous, they are not valuable ; their skins, however, might not form an unimportant article for export. Goats of a very fine and large kind are equally numerous, and sell at a lower price than sheep. Their skins are valuable. Pigs can be obtained in any numbers; they are kept at several of the coast stations. Domestic poultry, the Guinea hen, common fowls, ducks, &c., are literally swarming, especially in the interior, and may be had for the most trifling articles in barter both on the coast and inland. Fish of all kinds visit the shores and rivers in immense shoals, and are easily taken in great quantities during the proper season. The mineral kingdom has not yet been explored, but enough is already known to show that the precious metals abound, particularly gold. The gold-dust obtained from the beds of some rivers, and otherwise produced, is, comparatively, at present, a large branch of the African trade. It is said that gold may be procured in the kingdom of Bambouk, which is watered by the Felema, flowing into the Senegal, and is therefore easily attainable in any quantity. Martin says, (vol. iv., p. 540,) the main depositories where this metal is traced, as it were, to its source, are two mountains, Na Takon and Semayla. In the former, gold is very abundant, and is found united with earth, iron, or emery. In the latter, the gold is imbedded in hard sandstone. Numerous streams (he adds) flow from these districts, almost all of which flow over sands impregnated with gold. The natives, unskilled in mining operations, have penetrated to very little depth in these mountains. Park found the mines of the Konkadoo hills, which he visited, excessively rich, but very badly worked. (Chapter on gold, vol. i. pp. 454, 465, 524, and vol. ii., pp. 73, 76.) The gold which forms the staple commodity of the Gold Coast, is chiefly brought down from mountains of the interior. It is said that the whole soil yields gold-dust, and that small quantities are obtained even in the town of Cape Coast.* There are reported to be mines within twenty or thirty miles of the shore, but the natives are very jealous of allowing Europeans to see them.† Dupuis and Bowditch speak of the " solid lumps of rock gold" which ornament the persons of the cabooceers in the court of the king of Ashantee, at Coomassy.‡ Mrs. Lee (late Mrs. Bowditch) says, that the great men will frequently on state occasions, so load their wrists with these lumps, that they are obliged to support them on the head of a boy. The largest piece she saw at Cape Coast weighed 14 oz. and was very pure.§ Dupuis, on the authority of some Mohammedans, says that a great deal of gold

* Sierra Leone Report, 1830, p. 87.　　† Ib. p. 88.
‡ Dupuis' Ashantee, p. 74 ; Bowditch's Travels, p. 35.
§ " Stories of Strange Lands," p. 66.

comes from Gaman, and that it is the richest in Africa.* Gold is said to be discovered in a plain near Houssa ; and another writer (Jackson) says— " The produce of Soudan, returned by the akkabuahs, consists principally in gold-dust, twisted gold rings of Wangara, gold rings made at Sinnie (which are invariably of pure gold, and some of them of exquisite workmanship), bars of gold,† &c." He also states that gold-dust is the circulating medium at Timbuctoo.‡

Iron is found in Western Africa. The ore from Sierra Leone is particularly rich, yielding seventy-nine per cent., according to Mr. MacCormack, and said to be well adapted to making steel.§ The iron brought from Upper Senegal, by Mollien, was found to be of a very good quality. Berthier found it to resemble Catalonian.‖ Iron is found also near Timbuctoo, and is manufactured by the Arabs.¶ The discovery of this important metal in Africa, is of the utmost consequence to its future prosperity, and will greatly facilitate the accomplishment of the object contemplated. Early travellers relate that the mountains of Congo are almost all ferruginous, but that the natives have not been encouraged by Europeans to extract their own treasures. Copper is so abundant in Mayomba, that they gather from the surface of the ground enough for their purposes.** Sal ammoniac is found in abund-

---

* Dupuis, Ap. lvi.   † Jackson's Timbuctoo, p. 245, 246.
‡ Jackson's Timbuctoo, p. 251.   § Sierra Leone Report, 1830.
‖ Mollien's Travels, Appendix.   ¶ Jackson's Timbuctoo, p. 24.
** Degrandpré, T. F., p. 38.

ance in Dagwumba, and is sold cheap in the Ashantee market; nitre, emery, and trona, a species of
alkali, are found on the border of the Desert.* I might
greatly enlarge this list, from the writings of travellers who have already visited the country, but it will
be long before its mineral wealth will be adequately
known.

It is not, however, to the mineral treasures of
Africa that we chiefly look; we regard the productions of the soil as of infinitely more value, especially
those which require industry and skill in their
culture. We look to the forests, and the plains,
and the valleys, which it would take centuries to
exhaust of their fertility and products. The woods
of this continent are extremely valuable. Travellers
enumerate not less than forty species of timber, which
grow in vast abundance, and are easily obtained;
such as mahogany, teak, ebony, lignum vitæ, rose-
wood, &c.

While Colonel Nicolls was stationed at Fernando
Po, he gives this account of its timber, in a letter to
Mr. Secretary Hay. I extract the passage as a specimen of the nature of African forests. He says
that some of the trees are ten feet in diameter, and
120 feet in height.—" Twenty men have been for a
period of eight days cutting down one tree of these
dimensions, for the purpose of making a canoe; it
was quite straight without a branch; the wood
white in colour, close in grain, and very hard. I
have no name for it, but it very much resembles the

* Bowditch, p. 333.

lignum vitæ, except in colour. The canoe cut out of it is five feet within the gunwales, forty feet long, and carries about twenty tons safely, drawing but eight inches water. We have also a very fine description of red wood, close-grained, strong, and good for beams, sheathing, ribs, and deck-planking of the heaviest vessels of war. We could send home stern-posts and stems, in one piece, for the largest ships. This wood seems to have a grain something between mahogany and oak; when cut thin to mend boats, it will not split in the sun, and when tapped or cut down exudes a tough resinous gum, is very lasting, and not so heavy as teak or oak, takes a fine polish, and I think it a very valuable wood. There is another hard-wood tree of very large dimensions, the wood strong and good, in colour brown and white-streaked; it also exudes, when cut, a strong gum, which I think would be valuable in commerce. Another, which we call the mast-tree, from the circumstance of its being very tall and straight, is in colour and grain like a white pine. We have, besides the above-mentioned trees, many which are smaller, but very useful, their wood being hard, tough, and of beautifully variegated colours; some are streaked brown and white, like a zebra, others of black, deep red, and brown."

In a despatch, 1832, Colonel Nicolls further states, that he has Commodore Hayes' authority for saying, that there never was finer wood for the purposes of ship-building.*

* Desp. p. 5 ; Colonial Records, 1832.

Of dye-woods* there are also abundance, yielding
carmine, crimson, red, brown, brilliant yellow, and
the various shades from yellow to orange, and a fine

---

* Many beautiful kinds of wood have been discovered by accident amongst the billets of firewood, brought home in the slave-
ships to Liverpool.   Mr. Clarkson gives the following anecdote in
his " Impolicy of the Slave Trade."   After mentioning the tulip-
wood and others, found in this manner, he says :—" About the
same time in which this log was discovered (A. D. 1787), another
wood vessel, belonging to the same port, brought home the specimen of the bark of a tree, that produced a very valuable yellow
dye, and far beyond any other ever in use in this country.   The
virtues of it were discovered in the following manner :—A gentleman, resident upon the coast, ordered some wood to be cut down
to erect a hut.   While the people were felling it he was standing by; during the operation some juice flew from the bark of it
and stained one of the ruffles of his shirt.   He thought that the
stain would have washed out, but, on wearing it again, found that
the yellow spot was much more bright and beautiful than before,
and that it gained in lustre every subsequent time of washing.
Pleased with the discovery, which he knew to be of so much importance to the manufacturers of Great Britain, and for which a
considerable premium had been offered, he sent home the bark
now mentioned as a specimen.   He is since unfortunately dead,
and little hopes are to be entertained of falling in with this
tree again, unless a similar accident should discover it, or a
change should take place in our commercial concerns with
Africa.   I shall now mention another valuable wood, which,
like all those that have been pointed out, was discovered
by accident in the same year.   Another wood vessel, belonging
to the same port, was discharging her cargo ; among the barwood
a small billet was discovered, the colour of which was so superior
to that of the rest, as to lead the observer to suspect, that it was
of a very different species, though it is clear that the natives,
by cutting it of the same size and dimensions, and by bringing it
on board at the same time, had, on account of its red colour, mis-
taken it for the other.   One half of the billet was cut away in expe-
riments.   It was found to produce a colour that emulated the

blue. Of gums there are Copal, Senegal, Mastic, and Sudan, or Turkey gum, to be obtained in large quantities ; and there are forests near the Gambia where, hitherto, the gum has never been picked. Of nuts, which are beginning to form a new and important article of trade, there are the palm-nut, the shea-nut, the cola-nut, the ground-nut, the castor-nut, the nitta-nut, and the cocoa-nut. The palm-tree grows most luxuriantly, and incalculable quantities of its produce are allowed to rot on the ground for want of gathering ; yet it is now the most important branch of our commerce with Africa, and may be increased to any extent. The oil expressed from its nut is used in the manufacture of soap and candles, and in lubricating machinery. The shea, or butter-nut,* is scarcely less

carmine, and was deemed to be so valuable in the dyeing trade, that an offer was immediately made of sixty guineas per ton for any quantity that could be procured. The other half has been since sent back to the coast, as a guide to collect more of the same sort, though it is a matter of doubt whether, under the circumstances that have been related, the same tree can be ascertained again."—p. 9.

* The butter is prepared by boiling, and besides the advantage of keeping a whole year without salt, it is "whiter, firmer, and to my palate," says Park (vol. i. p. 302), " of a richer flavour than the best butter I ever tasted made of cow's milk." The shea tree, which produces it, is said to extend over a large part of the continent, from Jaloof to Gaboon. " It has been analysed by the French chemist, M. Chevreuil, and found well adapted for the manufacture of soap. Being inodorous and highly capable of taking a perfume, it would be valuable for the finer sorts."—Mrs. Lee, *Stories of Strange Lands*, p. 26.

valuable than the palm-nut. Some travellers inform their readers that it is an excellent substitute for butter, and can be appropriated to the same uses, with the palm-oil. It is a remarkable fact, in the natural history of these trees, that immediately where the one ceases to yield its fruit the other flourishes abundantly. The ground-nut* is becoming also a valuable article of commerce; and this with the other nuts mentioned, yield a rich supply of oil and oil-cake for the use of cattle. The value of the castor-nut, as an article of medicine, needs not be particularly adverted to. The roots which grow in Africa require generally but little attention in their cultivation; among others, there are the following:—The manioc, yams, sweet potatoes, arrow-root, and ginger :† the two latter are exportable, and the former yield a large amount of healthful and nutritious food. Yams can be so improved

---

* The *ground-nut* yields a pure golden-coloured oil, of a pleasant taste, and has been sold here at 56*l.* per ton. From 750 to 1000 tons are produced on the Gambia; but these nuts appear plentiful along the whole coast, are often mentioned by Park, and were noticed by Denham, as very abundant near the lake Tchad. It grows in a soil too light and sandy for corn—its stalks afford fodder for cattle—it sells at six shillings per gallon, and is as good as sperm-oil. The *castor-nut* also grows wild in great abundance on the banks of the Gambia, and elsewhere.

† The ginger of Africa is particularly fine, and high flavoured; it yields about sixty for one; and the people only want instruction in the method of preparing it for European markets.—*Denham, Desp.*, 21*st May*, 1827; *Sierra Leone Report*, 1830, *No.* 57, p. 30.

by cultivation that, at Fernando Po, Captain Bullen says, many weigh from fifteen to twenty-five pounds, and in taste almost equal a potato. On one occasion he bought upwards of four tons for seventy-six iron hoops, and says, " The nourishment derived from them to my people was beyond belief."* The fruits are oranges, lemons, citrons, limes, pines, guavas, tamarinds, paw-paws, plantains, and bananas. The paw-paw and plantain trees (says Ashmun) are a good example of the power of an uniformly-heated climate to accelerate vegetation. You may see in the gardens many of the former, not more than fifteen months from the seed, already fifteen inches round the stem, and fifteen feet high, with several pecks of ripening fruit. Clear your lands, plant your crops, keep the weeds down, and the most favourable climate in the world, alone, under the direction of a bountiful Providence, will do more for you than all your toil and care could accomplish in America."† Tamarinds are exportable. Of grain, there is rice, Indian corn, Guinea corn, or millet, &c. The quantities of these can be raised to any extent, and be limited only by demand.‡ The Rev. W. Fox, the

* Captain Bullen's Desp., November, 1826.

† Ashmun's Life, Ap. p. 66.

‡ " Nothing can be more delightful than a stroll along the borders of the beautiful fields, winding occasionally along almost impervious clusters of young palms, whose spreading branches excluded every ray of the scorching sun, then opening suddenly on an immense rice-field of the most delicate pea-green,

Missionary, says, in his MS. Journal, August 22, 1836 :—" This afternoon I visited Laming, a small Mandingo town (above Macarthy's Island). I could scarcely get into the town for the quantity of Indian corn with which it is surrounded : upon a very moderate calculation, and for a very small portion of labour, which generally devolves upon the poor women, they reap upwards of two hundred fold." I am informed that Madeira wholly depends on the maize raised in Africa, and that the rice produced there, when properly dried and prepared, is equal to that grown in South Carolina. Of drugs, there are aloes* and cassia, senna, frankincense, cardamons, and grains of paradise, or Malagetta pepper. Amongst the miscellaneous products, which are in great demand in this country, may be enumerated ivory, bees'-wax, caoutchouc, or Indian-rubber. The former of these articles will, of course, suffer a gradual diminution as the forests are cut down, the swamps drained, and the plains cultivated ; but of the latter scarcely any diminution need be apprehended. The bees'-wax of Africa is in great repute, and can be had in any quantity ; and the

---

skirted by the beautiful broad-leaved plantain and banana, literally groaning under the immense masses of their golden fruit."— Dr. J. Hall, Governor of Liberia. *Missionary Register*, 1836, p. 360.

* A new use of the aloe plant has been discovered, in the beautiful tissue and cordage manufactured from its fibres, by M. Pavy, of Paris. The fibres of the cocoa-nut might also be turned to account.

great price freely given for Indian-rubber might be a sufficient inducement to lead the African to pay more attention to its collection. Of this Mr. Rankin says,[*] describing what he saw in an excursion amongst the Timmanees,—" A large lump of Indian-rubber (caoutchouc) lay on the table, also the produce of Tombo. This article, at present acquiring a high value amongst our importations, is not there made an article of commerce. Like almost every other produce of the neighbourhood of Sierra Leone, it is scarcely known to exist, or is entirely neglected. It grows plentifully, and may be easily obtained by making incisions into the tree from which it flows, like cream, into calabashes tied underneath ; it hardens within a few hours."

There are some articles that require more notice : the chief of these is cotton. I have collected a great variety of authorities, all uniting in declaring that this plant grows wild in almost every part of Africa. Colonel Denham writes, that at Sierra Leone three sorts of cotton grow wild, white, brown, and pink ; the first excellent.[†] He also found it plentiful near lake Tchad[‡]. Ashmun says (Life, Ap. p. 76) that " the indigenous cotton plant of Liberia does not precisely answer to the American varieties, being of larger size and longer duration ;" but that " it is

---

[*] Rankin's Sierra Leone, vol. ii. p. 218.

[†] Denham, Despatch, 1827 ; Sierra Leone Report, 1830, No. 57, p. 30.

[‡] Denham, Travels, p. 317.

allowed on all hands to be of a good quality," and adds that weak upland soils will answer for this crop.

The culture of cotton is already so well understood in a country where nearly every person can weave, that little pains would suffice to bring it to perfection; it requires little capital, and affords a return the first year.

Hemp grows wild on the Gambia, and only requires a better mode of preparation to make it a valuable article of import. The same may be said of tobacco. Indigo grows so freely in Africa, that, in some places, it is difficult to eradicate it. " Immense quantities of indigo, and other noxious weeds," spring up in the streets of Freetown.*

It is known to grow wild as far inland as the Tchad, and even with the rude preparation bestowed by the natives, gives a beautiful dye to their cloths.†

Coffee is another indigenous shrub, which well repays cultivation. When Kizell, a Nova Scotian, first observed it near the Sherbro, he pulled up two or three plants, and showed them to the people, who said that they thought it was good for nothing, but to fence their plantations. It was all over the country, and in some places nothing else was to be seen.‡ Even in a wild state it seems to repay the trouble of gathering, for the Commissioners at Sierra

---

* Despatch, Mr. Smart to Sir G. Murray, 1828; Sierra Leone Report, No. 57, p. 30.

† Denham's Travels, p. 246.

‡ Afr. Inst. 6 Report, Ap.

Leone, in their Annual Report of date 1st January, 1838, inform us " that the Foulahs have been induced by the fair traders of the river Nunez to bring down for sale to them a quantity of coffee, of a very superior quality, the produce of the forests of their own country." An extract of a letter, which they enclose, observes that " one great advantage of peaceful commerce with the natives is, that valuable productions of their country are brought to light by our research, sometimes to their astonishment." Thus till within the last two years this abundant growth of coffee was " left to be the food of monkeys," but is now a source of profit to the natives, and to our own merchants. A small quantity has been cultivated, both at Sierra Leone and the Gold Coast; and Ashmun (Life, Ap. p. 78) states that, in Liberia, no crop is surer, that African coffee frequently produces four pounds to the tree, and that the berries attain a size unknown elsewhere. I am happy to learn that above 10,000 lbs. of African coffee were imported into this country in 1837, that its quality was excellent, and that it fetched a good price.*

Sugar-canes grow spontaneously in several parts

* Mr. M'Queen says, the old Arabian traveller Batouta, who had visited China, states, that in the interior parts of Africa, along the Niger, which he visited, the tea-plant grew abundantly.— M'Queen's *Africa*, p. 218. Dr. M'Leod, describing the kingdom of Benin, says: "In the opinion of one of the latest governors we have had on the establishment in this country (Mr. James), and one whose general knowledge of Africa is admitted to be considerable, the tea-tree flourishes spontaneously here."— M'Leod's *Voyage to Africa*, p. 18.

of Africa, and when cultivated, as they are in various places for the sake of the juice, they become very large. The expense of the necessary machinery alone seems to have hitherto prevented the manufacture of sugar; but, in fact, very little attention has yet been paid to the cultivation of the soil of Africa, though it is probable that hence would be derived the richest treasures of the country. Nearly all we know of its capabilities of improvement is from the rude efforts of negroes transported from North America, or liberated from slave-ships at Sierra Leone. What these men have wanted, as Colonel Denham remarks, is " instruction, example, and capital;" and he adds, " that, with the small amount of either that they have received, it is subject of astonishment to him that they have done what they have." (Despatch, May 21st, 1829.) They supply the market of Freetown with plenty of fruit and vegetables, such as yams, cassada, Indian corn, ground-nuts, pine-apples, sugar-canes, &c. &c.

Hitherto European settlers have been so occupied with trading, that they have paid scarcely any attention to agriculture; the want of proper superintendents has also been an obstacle to its pursuit, but it is thought that competent persons for this purpose might easily be procured from the West Indies.

Ashmun, who seems to have had a clear view of the interest of the Liberian settlers, writes to them thus:—" Suffer me to put down two or three remarks, of the truth and importance of which you cannot be too sensible. The first is, that the cultivation of your rich lands is the only way you will ever find out to independence, comfort, and wealth." "You may, if you please, if God gives you health, become as independent, comfortable, and happy as you ought to be in this world." "The flat lands around you, and particularly your farms, have as good a soil as can be met with in any country. They will produce two crops of corn, sweet potatoes, and several other vegetables in a year. They will yield a larger crop than the best soils in America. And they will produce a number of very valuable articles, for which in the United States, millions of money are every year paid away to foreigners. One acre of rich land, well tilled, will produce you three hundred dollars' worth of indigo. Half an acre may be made to grow half a ton of arrow-root. Four acres laid out in coffee-plants, will, after the third year, produce you a clear income of two or three hundred dollars. Half an acre of cotton-trees will clothe your whole family; and, except a little hoeing, your wife and children can perform the whole labour of cropping and manufacturing it. One acre of canes will make you independent of all the world, for the sugar you use in your family. One acre set with fruit-trees, and well attended, will furnish you the year round, with more plantains, bananas, oranges, limes, guavas, papaws, and pine-apples, than you will ever gather. Nine months of the year, you may grow fresh vegetables every month, and some of you who have lowland plantations, may do so throughout the year."*

3. Its rich alluvial deltas, and extensive and fertile plains, present a boundless field for cultivation.

Fifty miles to the leeward of the colony (Sierra Leone) is a vast extent of fertile ground, forming the delta of the Seeong Boom, Kitiam and Gallinas rivers. This ground may contain from 1000 to 1500 square miles of the richest alluvial soil, capable of growing all tropical produce. According to Mr. M'Cormack, this delta would grow rice enough for the supply of the whole West Indies.† At present it produces nothing but the finest description of slaves.‡

From Cape St. Paul to Cameroons, and from thence to Cape Lopez, extends the richest country that imagination can conceive. Within this space from forty to fifty rivers of all sizes discharge their waters into the ocean, forming vast flats of alluvial soil, to the extent of 180,000 square miles. From this ground at present the greatest amount of our imports from Western Africa is produced, and to it and the banks of the rivers that flow through it, do I look for the greatest and most certain increase of trade. It is a curious feature in the geography of Africa, that so many of its great navigable rivers

* Ashmun's Life, Ap. p. 64.

† Sierra Leone Report, No. 66, p. 64.

‡ There is another large delta, formed by the rivers Nunez, Rio Grande, and Rio Ponga. It is described as very extensive and fertile. The Isles de Loss command the mouths of these rivers. The Rio Nunez runs parallel with the Gambia.—Mr. Laird.

converge upon this point (Laird). The extent to which the Slave Trade is carried on in the rivers alluded to is immense, and offers the greatest possible obstruction to the fair trader.

With few inconsiderable exceptions, the whole line of coast in Western Africa, accessible to trading vessels, presents immense tracts of land of the most fertile character, which only require the hand of industry and commercial enterprise to turn them into inexhaustible mines of wealth.

But it is not to the coast alone that the commercial man may look for the results of his enterprise. The interior is represented as equally fertile with the coast ; and it is the opinion of the most recent travellers, as well as of those who preceded them, that if the labourer were allowed to cultivate the soil in security, the list of productions would embrace all the marketable commodities imported from the East and West Indies.

Between Kacunda and Egga, both large towns on the Niger, the country is described as very fertile, and from Egga to Rabbah, where the river is 3000 yards wide, the right bank is represented to consist of extensive tracts of cultivated land, with rich and beautiful plains stretching as far as the eye could reach (Laird). The country does not deteriorate as we ascend the river. We have the testimony of Park corroborated by Denham and Clapperton, in support of this statement, and their remarks embrace both sides of the river. The country surrounding Cape Palmas, the Gambia, the Senegal, the Shary, the Congo, presents to the eye of the traveller unlimited tracts of the most fertile portion of the earth.

It is observed by Brown, in his botanical appendix to "Tuckey's Voyage" (pp. 342, 3), that from the river Senegal, in about 16° north latitude, to the Congo, in upwards of 6° south latitude, there is a remarkable uniformity in the vegetation of Western Africa—a fact which gives us promise of extending to any amount our commerce in such vegetable productions as have already obtained a sale in Europe or America. Thus a tree which characterises nearly the whole range of coast, is the Elais Guineensis, or oil-palm, one of the most valuable to commerce. This grows in the greatest abundance in the delta of the Niger. There "the palm-nut now rots on the ground unheeded and neglected," over an extent of surface equal to the whole of Ireland. (Laird, vol. ii. p. 362.)

The whole extent too of the Timmanee, and a great part of Koranko, through which Captain Laing passed in 1822, was absolutely bristled with palm-trees, which at the time he went up the country (April and May) were bearing luxurious crops of nuts. "There is no known instance, or any apparent danger, of a failure on the part of all-bountiful nature in supplying the fruit; on the contrary, it is the opinion of Captain Laing, that were the population double, and had they all the industry we could wish, they would not be able to reap the abundant harvest annually presented to them."*

The soil of Africa produces indigenously nearly

* Sierra Leone Gaz., Dec. 14, 1822.

all the useful plants which are common to other tropical countries, and some of them in greater perfection than they are to be found elsewhere.

Its mighty rivers and their tributary streams, navigable to immense distances from the coast, and communicating with the nations of the interior, present unlimited facilities for commercial intercourse.

The number and situation of the navigable rivers on the western coast of Africa have often been the subject of remark by those who have visited them, and particularly as affording the noblest means for extending the commerce of this country to the millions who dwell on their banks, or occupy the cities and towns in the interior. Along the coast, commencing at the southern point of the Bight of Biafra, and embracing the coast of Calabar, the Slave Coast, the Gold Coast, the Ivory Coast, the Grain Coast, the Pepper Coast, the coast of Sierra Leone, and thence northwards to the Senegal, there cannot be less than ninety or one hundred rivers, many of them navigable, and two of them rivalling in their volume of water and extent the splendid rivers of North America. It is reported that a French steam-vessel plies more than 700 miles up the Senegal, and that the Faleme, which flows into it eight leagues below Galam, is navigable in the rainy season for vessels of sixty tons burden. The Faleme runs through the golden land of Bambouk, whence the French traders obtain considerable quantities of that precious metal. The Gambia is a noble river. It is about eleven miles wide at its mouth, and about four opposite Bathurst. How far it extends into the interior is unknown; it is said, however, that it has been ascended for some hundred miles.* It is also asserted, that from the upper part of this river the Senegal can be reached in three, and the Niger in four days. The Niger offers an uninterrupted passage to our steam-boats for 560 miles inland; and there is every probability that, with the exception perhaps of one or two portages, water-carriage might be gained to a length of 2500 miles further; and also that the Tchadda, which falls into the Niger, would open up a ready communication with all the nations inhabiting the unknown countries between the Niger and the Nile. It would be impossible to enumerate the powerful kingdoms in central Africa, which can be reached by the Niger and its tributary streams; but they are represented by various travellers as easy of access, abounding with the elements of commerce, populous, and rich in grain, fruits, cattle, and minerals.

In addition to the mighty rivers above referred to, it has been ascertained that, from Rio Lagos to the

---

* In 1834, Captain Quin carried Governor Randall up to Macarthy's island, in the Britomart sloop-of-war. Craft of 50 or 60 tons can get up to Fattatenda, the resort of caravans for trade with British merchants. Commodore Owen terms the Gambia "a magnificent river." It was surveyed in 1826 by Lieutenant Owen, R.N., on which occasion he was accompanied by the Acting Governor Macaulay, as far as Macarthy's island, 180 miles up the river.—Owen, ii. p. 373.

river Elrei, no fewer than twenty streams enter the ocean, several of surprising magnitude, and navigable for ships (M'Queen) ; and that all the streams which fall into the sea from Rio Formosa to Old Calabar inclusive are connected together by intermediate streams, at no great distance from the sea, and so may be said to be the mouths of the Niger (Leonard, p. 20).

Its industrial resources is another feature demanding serious attention. By these I mean not merely its extreme fertility, and capabilities for the most extended cultivation and commerce, but the activity and enterprise of its people. On the coast there is a belt of slave-trading chiefs, who, at present, find it more profitable to supply the slave-markets than to conduct a legitimate commerce. Little business can be done when there are any slavers at their stations, —indeed, the fair traders are always compelled to wait until the human cargoes are completed. These chiefs not only obstruct the fair trader on the coast, but as much as possible prevent his access to the interior.* Insecurity, demoralization, and degrada-

* The blighting effect of the Slave Trade on the well-being of the natives needs no proof; but it appears from the reports of early travellers, that they were once in a much less wretched condition than that in which they are now found. Traces are yet to be seen of cultivation which has once existed. Thus Ashmun, after a voyage which he made in 1822 for 200 miles to the south-eastward from Cape Montserado, remarks, "One century ago, a great part of this line of coast was populous, cleared of trees, and under cultivation. It is now covered with a dense and almost continuous forest. This is almost wholly a second growth,

tion are the results; but as you recede from the coast, and ascend the rivers, comparative civilization exists, industry becomes apparent, and no inconsiderable skill in many useful arts is conspicuous. All travellers have observed the superior cultivation, and comparatively dense population of the inland regions. Laird, in ascending the Niger, writes, "Both banks of the river are thickly studded with towns and villages; I could count seven from the place where we lay aground; and between Eboe and the confluence of the rivers there cannot be less than forty, one generally occurring every two or three miles. The principal towns are Attah and Addakudda; and averaging the inhabitants at 1000, will, I think, very nearly give

commonly distinguished from the original by the profusion of brambles and brushwood which abounds amongst the larger trees, and renders the woods entirely impervious, even to the natives, until paths are opened by the bill-hook."—Life of Ashmun, p. 141.

Speaking of the St. Paul's, he says, " Along this beautiful river were formerly scattered, in Africa's better days, innumerable native hamlets; and till within the last twenty years, nearly the whole river-board, for one to two miles back, was under that slight culture which obtains among the natives of this country. But the population has been wasted by the rage for trading in slaves; with which the constant presence of slaving-vessels, and the introduction of foreign luxuries has inspired them. The south bank of this river, and all the intervening country between it and the Montserado, have been, from this cause, nearly desolated of inhabitants."—p. 233.

The kingdoms of Whydah and Ardrah are represented to have been like a garden covered with fruits and grain of every description, until they were devastated by the slave-hunting Dahomey. Martin, vol. iv. p. 231.

the population of the banks." * * * "The
general character of the people is much superior to
that of the swampy country between them and the
coast. They are shrewd, intelligent, and quick in
their perception, milder in their disposition, and
more peaceable in their habits." Oldfield says
(vol. i. p. 163), that, from the great number of towns
they passed, he is inclined to suppose that the population must be very dense indeed. And (vol. ii. p.
17) "no sooner does the traveller approach one town,
than he discovers three or four, and sometimes five
others." Park speaks (vol. ii. p. 80) of the " hills
cultivated to the very summit, and the surplus grain
employed in purchasing luxuries from native traders."
Laing speaks (p. 156) with delight of " the extensive
meadows, clothed in verdure, and the fields from which
the springing rice and ground-nuts were sending forth
their green shoots, not inferior in beauty and health
to the corn-fields of England, interspersed here and
there with a patch of ground studded with palm-
trees." Tuckey reports (p. 342) a similar improvement
in the face of the country at some distance up the
Congo, where he found towns and villages following
each other in rapid succession. Ashmun, writing from
Liberia, says, " An excursion of some of our people
into the country, to the distance of about 140 miles,
has led to a discovery of the populousness and comparative civilization of this district of Africa, never
till within a few months even conjectured by myself.
We are situated within fifty leagues of a country, in

Q

which a highly improved agriculture prevails; where
the horse is a common domestic animal, where extensive tracts of land are cleared and enclosed, where
every article absolutely necessary to comfortable life
is produced by the skill and industry of the inhabitants; where the Arabic is used as a written language
in the ordinary commerce of life; where regular and
abundant markets and fairs are kept; and where a
degree of intelligence and practical refinement distinguishes the inhabitants, little compatible with the
personal qualities attached, in the current notions of
the age, to the people of Guinea."*

The wants of the people in Africa must not, any
more than their industry and enterprise, be judged
by what is observable on the coast. The Moors,
who have preceded us in the interior, have imparted
more knowledge than we may suppose of commercial
transactions. Captain Clapperton told Mr. Hamilton
that he could have negotiated a bill on the Treasury
of London at Socatoo. The Moors have introduced
the use of the Arabic in mercantile affairs; and that
language is nearly as useful in Africa as the French
language is in Europe. In 1812, Mr. Willis, formerly British Consul for Senegambia, stated his belief
that in the warehouses of Timbuctoo were accumu-
lated the manufactures of India and Europe, and that
the immense population of the banks of the Niger
are thence supplied. A Moorish merchant reported
to Mr. Jackson, that between Mushgrelia and Houssa,

* From Miss. Regr. for 1828, p. 335.

there were more boats employed on the river, than between Rosetta and Cairo ; and that the fields of that country were enclosed and irrigated by canals and water-wheels,*—a demonstrative proof of the activity, industry, and civilization of the people.

" Thirty years' experience," says an African merchant (Mr. Johnston), " of the natives, derived from living amongst them for the whole of that period, leaves a strong impression on my mind that, with due encouragement, they would readily be led to the cultivation of the soil, which I think in most places capable of growing anything." Mr. Laird, in a letter to me, observes,—"As to the character of the inhabitants, I can only state that, if there is one characteristic that distinguishes an African from other uncivilised people, it is his love of, and eagerness for, traffic : men, women, and children trade in all directions. They have regular market-places where they bring the produce of their fields, their manufactures, their ivory, and everything they can sell." * * * " At the Iccory-Market I have seen upwards of one hundred large canoes, each holding from ten to forty men, all trading peaceably together. I was informed by the natives that it was considered neutral ground, and that towns at war with one another attended the same market amicably." The industrious inhabitants of the Grain Coast supply Sierra Leone and Liberia with the greatest portion of their food.

Nearly the same account may be given of the exu-

* Jackson's Timbuctoo, pp. 24, 38, and 427.

berant fertility of the eastern as of the western coast, and of the lucrative character of the commerce which might be there carried on were it not for the destructive Slave Trade. I have been informed, by the captain of a merchant-vessel who was long on the eastern coast, that before the Slave Trade absorbed the whole attention of the people, two merchant-ships used to be annually despatched from Lisbon, which for the most paltry outfit brought home return cargoes of from 40,000*l.* to 60,000*l.**

Other testimonies might be added to show that the African is not wanting in those qualities which accompany civilization, and that he only requires a right direction to be given to his industry and intelligence to qualify him for intercourse with the more refined European.

The eagerness with which the Timmanees entered into the laborious and fatiguing work of cutting, squaring, and floating to the trading stations, the immense bodies of heavy teak timber exported from Sierra Leone, is a convincing proof of their readi-

* The gentleman who furnished this information, mentions the following articles of commerce on the eastern coast of Africa:— Gold, silver, copper, iron, ivory, horns, tallow, hides, skins, tortoiseshell, ostrich-feathers, pearls, ambergris, amber, gums and various drugs, palm-oil, cocoa-nut oil, black whale oil, sperm-oil, bees'-wax in great abundance, coffee, tobacco, indigo, corn, rice, &c. A most profitable trade might also be carried on in cowries, which abound on the coast, where he has purchased them at 4*d.* a-bushel; on the western coast they are the current coin, and are told out by the hundred. All these articles find a ready market at Ceylon, Bombay, and Calcutta.

ness to engage in any employment where they can get a reward, however small, for their labour. It is well known that during the time the timber trade was in activity, several native towns were formed on the banks of the river, and many natives came from a distance in the country to engage in it. Timber was cut at the termination of the largest creeks at Port Logo, and even so far as Rokou, and floated down to Tombo, Bance Island, and Tasso. (Laing, p. 77.)*

I have lately seen a portion of the Journal of the Rev. W. Fox, written at Macarthy's Island, in which, of date September 3, 1836, he mentions having given away a considerable number of Arabic Scriptures to Mandingoes, and to Serrawoollies, or Tiloboonkoes, as they are here more generally termed; which lite-rally means eastern people, as they come from the neighbourhood of, and beyond, Bondou, and are strict Mahommetans. They come here and hire themselves as labourers for several months, and with the articles they receive in payment barter them again on their way home for more than their actual value on this island.

* " Twenty years ago," says Laird (vol. ii. p. 363), " African timber was unknown in the English market. There are now from 13,000 to 15,000 loads annually imported. In 1832 Mr. Forster, in a letter to Lord Goderich, stated the importation as high as ' from 15,000 to 20,000 loads, giving employment to 20,000 tons of shipping annually.' From 3000 to 4000 loads of red teak-wood are exported annually from the Gambia," and the mahogany from that river is now much used for furniture.

The Kroomen who inhabit Cape Palmas are a most extraordinary race of men. They neither sell nor allow themselves to be made slaves. These men leave their homes young, and work on board the trading vessels on the coast, or at Sierra Leone. Their attachment to their country is great, nor will they engage themselves for more than three years. "To my mind," says Mr. Laird, in the letter to me which I have before quoted, "these men appear destined by Providence to be the means of enabling Europeans to penetrate into the remotest parts of Africa by water. They are patient, enduring, faithful, easily kept in order, and brave to rashness when led by white men. Any number may be got at wages from two to four dollars per month."

We thus find that little difficulty exists in procuring either labourers or seamen in Africa.

From the foregoing remarks it is quite clear that the present commercial intercourse between this country and Africa is extremely limited; that the chief obstacle to its extension is the prevalence of the Slave Trade,* and that it might be indefinitely

---

* The imports of palm-oil have diminished during the last four years, as may be seen by the following returns, viz. :—

			Cwts.
1834	.	.	269,907
1835	.	.	234,882
1836	.	.	236,195
1837	.	.	201;906

This diminution has arisen, not in consequence of a decrease in the demand for the article, but on account of the extension of the

increased under the fostering and protective care of the British government. The grounds on which this supposition rests are the number and situation of its navigable rivers ; its rich alluvial deltas, and extensive and fertile plains ; its immense forests ; its wide range of natural productions ; its swarming, active, and enterprising population ; its contiguity to Europe, and the demand of its people for the manufactures of this country.

In speculating on African commerce, it should be borne in mind that we have to deal with nations who are not only ignorant and uncivilised, but cor-

Slave Trade on the coast, and the increased difficulty of procuring a supply.

" The industry of the natives, in a great degree, is stifled by the Slave Trade ; and, though a good deal of oil is prepared and sold, the English traders, loading at the mouth of the river, are often interrupted, and obliged to wait, to the loss of profit and the ruin of the crew's health, while a smuggling slaver takes all hands on the coast to complete her cargo."—*Laird.*

" When there is a demand for slaves the natives abandon every other employment ; and the consequence is, that the British vessels trading on the coast are lying idle for want of trade."

" In consequence of the great demand for slaves, the natives here and in the interior abandon cultivation, the trees go to destruction, and no young trees are planted."—*Extract from recent Letters from Africa which have been shown to me.*

By the latest intelligence we are informed " that at one place in Africa where a very considerable quantity of palm-oil has been annually supplied to the ships of our merchants, the Spanish and Portuguese have latterly so much increased the Slave Trade, that the cultivation of the palm-trees, which was giving occupation to thousands, has not only become neglected, but the native chiefs have been incited to blind revenge against British influence, and have set fire to and destroyed 30,000 palm-trees."

rupted and deteriorated by the Slave Trade and intercourse with the worst class of Europeans. There will, therefore, be difficulties and obstructions to overcome before a clear field for honest commerce can be obtained. In the present state of the people we can hardly look to obtain from them articles which depend on an extensive cultivation of the soil, so as to compete with the productions of civilised nations. It is probable that in commencing an extensive intercourse with Africa there will be at first a considerable outlay of money without an immediate return; but, from whatever source this may be obtained, it should be considered as a gift to Africa. It will ultimately be repaid a thousand-fold.

The articles desired by the Africans in return for the produce of their country are too many to enumerate. Lists of them are given by almost every traveller. It may, therefore, suffice to observe, that many of them are the produce or manufactures of our island or of our colonies; and it is an important consideration, that we may obtain the treasures of this unexplored continent, by direct barter of our own commodities, and that, while we cheapen luxuries at home, we also increase the means of obtaining them, by giving increased employment to our productive classes.

The extension of a legitimate commerce, and with it the blessings of civilization and Christianity, is worthy the most strenuous exertions of the philanthropist, whilst to the mercantile and general interests of the civilised world it is of the highest importance. Africa presents an almost boundless tract of country, teeming with inhabitants who admire, and are desirous of possessing, our manufactures. There is no limit to the demand, except their want of articles to give us in return. They must be brought to avail themselves of their own resources.

Attempts have, as we have seen, already been made to form cotton plantations, and the article produced is found to be of a very useful and valuable description. Perseverance in these efforts is alone required to accomplish the object in view, and, when once accomplished, the importance to this country will be incalculable. The trade in palm-oil is capable of immense extension, and the article is every year becoming more important and in more extensive use. In exchange for these, and many other valuable articles, British manufactures would be taken, and British ships find a profitable employment in the conveyance of them.

It so happens that a considerable proportion of the goods which best suit the taste of the natives of Africa consists of fabrics to which power-looms cannot be applied with any advantage. Any extension, then, of the trade to Africa, will have this most important additional advantage, that it will cause a corresponding increase in the demand for the labour of a class of individuals who have lately been truly represented as suffering greater privations than any other set of workmen connected with the cotton trade.

But the first object of our intercourse with Africa

should be, not so much to obtain a remunerating trade as to repair in some measure the evil that the civilised world has inflicted on her, by conveying Christianity, instruction, and the useful arts to her sons. The two objects will eventually, if carried on in a right manner, be found perfectly compatible ; for it is reasonable to seek in legitimate commerce a direct antidote to the nefarious traffic which has so long desolated and degraded her. We have shown the vast variety and importance of the pro- ductions which Africa is capable of yielding ; we have already proved that, notwithstanding the bounty of nature, the commerce of Africa is most insignifi- cant. Truly may we say with Burke, " To deal and traffic—not in the labour of men, but in men them- selves—is to devour the root, instead of enjoying the fruit, of human diligence."

This work has been divided into two portions. The first is a description of Africa, as it now is. The second is intended to show what it might be- come, if its capabilities were turned to a good ac- count. I shall conclude with a few observations on these two points.

Towards the end of the last century the cruelty and the carnage which raged in Africa were laid open. From the most generous motives, and at a mighty cost, we have attempted to arrest this evil ; it is, however, but too evident, that, under the mode we have taken for the suppression of the Slave Trade, it has increased.

It has been proved, by documents which cannot be controverted, that, for every village fired and every drove of human beings marched in former times, there are now double. For every cargo then at sea, two cargoes, or twice the numbers in one cargo, wedged together in a mass of living corruption, are now borne on the wave of the Atlantic. But, whilst the numbers who suffer have increased, there is no reason to believe that the sufferings of each have been abated; on the contrary, we know that in some particulars these have increased; so that the sum total of misery swells in both ways. Each individual has more to endure; and the number of individuals is twice what it was. The result, therefore, is, that aggravated suffering reaches multiplied numbers.

It is hardly necessary to remind the reader that the statement I have given of the enormities attendant on the supply of slaves to the New World must, from the nature of the case, be a very faint picture of the reality—a sample, and no more, of what is inflicted and endured in Africa. Our knowledge is very limited; but few travellers have visited Africa —the Slave Trade was not their object, and they had slender means of information beyond what their own eyes furnished; yet, what do they disclose?

If Africa were penetrated in every direction by persons furnished with the means of obtaining full and correct information, and whose object was the delineation of the Slave Trade—if, not some isolated spots, but the whole country, were examined—if, instead of a few casual visitors, recording the events of to-day, but knowing nothing of what occurred yesterday, or shall take place to-morrow, we had everywhere those who would chronicle every slave-hunt, and its savage concomitants ;—if we thus possessed the means of measuring the true breadth and depth of this trade in blood, — is it not fair to suppose that a mass of horrors would be collected, in comparison with which all that has been hitherto related would be as nothing ?

It should be borne in constant memory, difficult as it is to realise—That the facts I have narrated are not the afflictions of a narrow district, and of a few inhabitants ;—the scene is a quarter of the globe—a multitude of millions its population —That these facts are not gleaned from the records of former times, and preserved by historians as illustrations of the strange and prodigious wickedness of a darker age. They are the common occurrences of our own era —the " customs" which prevail at this very hour. Every day which we live in security and peace at home witnesses many a herd of wretches toiling over the wastes of Africa, to slavery or death ; every night villages are roused from their sleep, to the alternatives of the sword, or the flames, or the manacle.   At the time I am writing there are at least *twenty thousand human beings* on the Atlantic, exposed to every variety of wretchedness which belongs to the middle passage.   Well might Mr. Pitt say, "there is something in the horror of it which surpasses all the bounds of imagination."

I do not see how we can escape the conviction that such is the result of our efforts, unless by giving way to a vague and undefined hope, with no evidence to support it, that the facts I have collected, though true at the time, are no longer a fair exemplification of the existing state of things. After I had finished my task, and on the day when I had intended to send this work to the press, I was permitted to see the most recent documents relating to the Slave Trade. In these I find no ground for any such consolatory surmise ; on the contrary, I am driven by them to the sorrowful conviction, that the year, from September, 1837, to September, 1838, is distinguished beyond all preceding years for the extent of the trade, for the intensity of its miseries, and for the unusual havoc it makes on human life.

If I believed that the evil, terrible as it is, were also irremediable, I should be more than ready to bury this mass of distress, and this dark catalogue of crime, in mournful silence, and to spare others, and especially those who have sympathised with, and laboured for, the negro race, from sharing with me the pain of learning how wide of the truth are the expectations in which we have indulged. But I feel no such despondency ; I firmly believe that Africa has within herself the means and the endowments which might enable her to shake off, and to emerge from, her load of misery, to the benefit of the whole civilised world, and to the unspeakable improvement of her own, now barbarous population.   This leads me to the second point, viz., the capabilities of Africa.

There are two questions which require to be decided before we can assume that it is possible to extinguish the Slave Trade.   First, Has Africa that latent wealth, and those unexplored resources, which would, if they were fully developed, more than compensate for the loss of the traffic in man ?   Secondly, Is it possible so to call forth her capabilities, that her natives may perceive that the Slave Trade, so far from being the source of their wealth, is the grand barrier to their prosperity, and that by its suppression they would be placed in the best position for obtaining all the commodities and luxuries which they are desirous to possess ?   With respect to the last of these propositions, I am of opinion that the time has not yet arrived when it would be expedient to publish, in detail, the measures which, according to my view, are necessary, in order that the African may be taught to explore the wealth of his exuberant soil, and to enjoy the sweets of legitimate commerce.   These views have been communicated to Her Majesty's Government.   It is for them to decide how far they are safe, practicable, and effectual. When their decision shall have been made, there will be no occasion for any farther reserve.   The second portion of this work will then be published, in which it is my purpose to say something on the geography of Africa ; something on the moral degradation and cruel superstitions which prevail among its population ; and something on the measures necessary for elevating the native mind. To these I shall add suggestions of the practical means which appear to me best calculated for the deliverance of Africa from the Slave Trade.

But the former question remains. Is Africa (if justice shall be done to her) capable of yielding a richer harvest than that which has been hitherto reaped from the sale and the slaughter of her people?

Beyond all doubt, she has within herself all that is needed for the widest range of commerce, and for the most plentiful supply of everything which conduces to the comfort and to the affluence of man. Her soil is eminently fertile.* Are its limits narrow? It stretches from the borders of the Mediterranean to the Cape of Good Hope, and from the Atlantic to the Indian Ocean. Are its productions such as we little want or lightly value? The very commodities most in request in the civilised world are the spontaneous growth of these uncultivated regions. Is the interior inaccessible? The noblest rivers flow through it, and would furnish a cheap and easy mode of conveyance for every article of legitimate trade. Is there a dearth of population, or is that population averse to the the pursuits of commerce? Drained of its inhabitants as Africa has been, it possesses an enormous population, and these eminently disposed to traffic. Does it lie at so vast a distance as to forbid the hope of continual intercourse? In sailing to India we

---

* Ptolemy says it " is richer in the quality, and more wonderful in the quantity, of its productions, than Europe or Asia."

pass along its western and eastern coasts. In comparison with China, it is in our neighbourhood.

Are not these circumstances sufficient to create the hope that Africa is capable of being raised from her present abject condition, and while improving her own state, of adding to the enjoyments and stimulating the commerce of the civilised world?

It is earnestly to be desired that all Christian powers should unite in one great confederacy, for the purpose of calling into action the dormant energies of Africa; but if this unanimity is not to be obtained, there are abundant reasons to induce this nation, alone if it must so be, to undertake the task. Africa and Great Britain stand in this relation toward each other. Each possesses what the other requires, and each requires what the other possesses. Great Britain wants raw material, and a market for her manufactured goods. Africa wants manufactured goods, and a market for her raw material. Should it, however, appear that, in place of profit, loss were to be looked for, and obloquy instead of honour, I yet believe that there is that commiseration, and that conscience in the public mind, which will induce this country to undertake, and with the Divine blessing enable her to succeed in crushing " the greatest practical evil that ever afflicted mankind."*

* Mr. Pitt.

London: Printed by W. Clowes and Sons, Stamford Street.

For EU product safety concerns, contact us at Calle de José Abascal, 56–1°, 28003 Madrid, Spain or eugpsr@cambridge.org.